The Bible:

WHY TRUST IT?

The Bible:

WHY TRUST IT?

by

I. Mac Perry

aven books
Division of Logos International
Plainfield, N.J. 07060

All Scripture references are from the King James Version, unless otherwise indicated TLB (*The Living Bible*) or RSV (Revised Standard Version).

*To Johnny, Derek,
Teague, and Clay*

Contents

Preface

As a young boy I grew up in a Christian home. I learned the stories of Jesus. "Scenes by the wayside, tales of the sea, stories of Jesus" were told to me. And I believed them—a Savior sent into the world to shed His blood that I might have everlasting life.

But as I entered the audience of the intellectually enlightened—college—my foundation of faith began to crack under pressure. I remembered how with sadness I had released Superman and Santa Claus to a youthful world of make-believe. Was I now to release my last treasure chest of hope—a loving God who had created me and placed me in a beautiful world; a God who sent His only Son to show me the truth about life and set me free from the fear of death's cold veil; a God who left me an amazing Book that reveals untold secrets about His Son, mankind, the future, and how I can live forever?

My Christian belief was being put to a crucial test. It was to be sifted through the fine-mesh sieve of reason I had developed from a quarter of a century of life in an educated society. I knew that the Christian foundation I had developed as a child would not withstand the load about to be dumped on by peer pressure, respected professors, scientific journals, and scholarly texts. If God was for real, He would have to show me something more than Jesus sitting on a rock telling stories to little children. God would have to bear the load. If He was real, He would pass through the sieve of reason with no impurities screened out. I was willing to be the sieve and subject myself to man-concocted, theorized speculations about life and the biblical account of life.

It has now been ten years since my study began, and I can say without any pretense that Christianity—the belief that Jesus of Nazareth is the begotten Son of God whose sinless life, crucifixion, and subsequent resurrection grants everlasting life to all who believe in Him—is the most credible, logical, reasonable revelation of truth to be found on earth. God and all teachings of His Holy Bible pass effortlessly through the sieve of reason. There is nothing more solid, sound, or stable than the Christian belief. To all who seek, God will reinforce their foundation of faith with such invulnerability that no theory, hypothesis, or concoction devised by man will even taint it, much less crack it.

Here in this volume I offer some of the facts God has given us to stabilize the credibility of Christianity. I would hope as you compare this text with the Scriptures you will turn to God and say, along with a multitude of men and women set free, "Yes, Lord, I believe."

Mac Perry

The Bible:
WHY TRUST IT?

PART ONE

THAT AMAZING BOOK, THE BIBLE

Before the Bible can be trusted as the words of God it must first prove itself to come from God. Could man alone have written the Bible? Does the Bible possess a nature beyond man? Search the Bible yourself and see what millions have discovered. See . . .

Why the Bible Is So Amazing

The Bible is our guide to perfect happiness and peace both on earth and after death. How do I know that? Because the Bible comes from God. There is abundant evidence to justify this statement.

The Bible briefly describes the entire history of man on earth, from Eden to Armageddon. But before we can search the Bible for the existence of God, proof of the deity of Jesus, the way to receive eternal life, and the secret of living in perfect joy and abundance, we must acknowledge one fact: *the Bible is all truth.* Until we decide for ourselves that we can believe the Bible because it comes from God and is all true, then it will be very hard to discover God in the Bible. Here are six facts that can help us accept the Bible as the Word of God.

1. Perfect Consistency from Imperfect Men
The Bible is not one but actually a collection of sixty-six books written over a period of 1600 years by forty different authors. Each writer wrote under God's inspiration (2 Tim. 3:16). The subjects include law, history, philosophy, poetry, prophecy, biographies, Christian doctrine, and revelations of things to come. The Old

Testament was written mostly in Hebrew (a few portions are in Aramaic), while the New Testament was written in Greek.

Some of the authors were well-learned men (Isaiah and Paul); others were common fishermen (Peter and John). Some were kings and wrote from palaces (David and Solomon), while others wrote from prison (Paul to the Ephesians). There were statesmen (Isaiah), priests (Samuel), warriors (Joshua), a Gentile doctor (Luke), a Pharisee (Paul), and several apostles (John, Matthew, Peter). The Bible possesses an infinite variety of themes and styles. Some are highlights written in haste (Mark), others carefully researched (Luke).

Out of all this diversity, the miracle is that there is *perfect consistency of thought*. It is impossible to have any two *qualified* men write on any one subject today without disagreement, much less forty apparently *unqualified* men over a 1600-year period. Yet when there is one author, God, to inspire the thoughts of His writers, unity prevails. Throughout the Bible we find the central theme of man's fall into sin and God's solution (Jesus) to redeem him out of darkness and into light. Never once do these authors claim to write their own thoughts, but over 2000 times they claim to be writing the words of God, as they use such phrases as, "thus saith the Lord." Surely this miracle alone gives us the right to say the Bible is the work of God. But there is more.

2. *Those Amazing Prophecies*

Over one-sixth of the Bible is prophecy, predictions made about future events. The test of a prophet of God, as described by Moses, is that every prediction must come true exactly as stated (Deut. 18:22). This has been the case in hundreds of prophecies given by men of the Bible speaking God's words. Concerning Jesus alone there were over 300 predictions made about Him long before He was ever born. *Every one of them came true just as stated.* Here are just a few of these amazing predictions.

Isaiah was a statesman who lived in Jerusalem 700 years before Jesus was born. He had a wife and two children, and they served over forty years under the reign of four kings. Isaiah stated that Jesus would be born of a virgin (7:14), He would be a descendant of David (9:7), He would lead the life of a good shepherd (40:11), he would heal the blind, the deaf, the lame, and the dumb (35:5) and Isaiah told us the government would be upon His shoulders and that He would be called the Prince of Peace (9:6). This prophet Isaiah also gave the world a glimpse of the crucifixion, that Jesus would be despised and rejected and men would turn their backs on Him, yet it was our grief and our sorrows He would bear. He would be wounded (side pierced) and bruised (beaten) and whipped (thirty-nine times). God would lay *our* guilt on Him. He would stand silent before His accusers (during the trials). He would be buried like a criminal but in a rich man's grave (Joseph of Arimathea). Yet He would have a multitude of children (Christians) and He would live again. All of these prophecies are found in the fifty-third chapter of Isaiah.

Today, we know all of these and numerous other Messianic prophecies given by Isaiah and other prophets *all* came true just as they gave them. The probability that all of the more than twenty-one prophecies about Jesus could come true exactly as stated, assuming a fifty-fifty chance for each prophecy, is one chance in 2,097,152 (two to the twenty-first power). Though the odds were over two mllion to one *against* them all coming true, *every one was fulfilled.* Surely these are the words of God and not Isaiah.

3. The Bible and Science

The Bible is not a science book. Often we try to make it one. Answers are not given to all the many puzzles of life we observe around us. God allows man to unfold these one at a time. However, in God's Bible the writers, while recording their inspirations, often wrote scientific thought without knowing it.

For example, contemporary medical research has told us that the life of man is in his blood. God told us this 2500 years ago in explaining that it is the blood that atones for the soul (Lev. 17:11). That, of course, is why Jesus had to lose blood on the cross in order for man's sin to be pardoned.

Columbus, in the fifteenth century, set out to prove the earth was round. But 2200 years before Columbus, Someone inspired Isaiah to write that God "sitteth upon the *circle* of the earth" (40:22), implying the earth is round.

For centuries it was believed that the earth sat upon a pedestal. But the book of Job, perhaps the oldest book of the Bible, records that God "hangeth the earth upon nothing" (26:7).

Early astronomers counted the stars of the heavens and for years published this number. But Jeremiah was inspired long before them to say the stars "cannot be numbered" (33:22). And Paul, writing in the first century, told us that all the stars are different long before science affirmed this (1 Cor. 15:41). Surely these words must have come from a source greater than man, a source whose perspective must have been equal to God himself.

4. *The Miracle of Bible Survival*

For 3500 years the Bible has been a best seller. No committee or organization ever sat down and said which books were to be in the Bible. The first-century church had numerous letters and writings. By the end of the second century, under the direction of divine providence and selection from numerous churches separated by hundreds of miles, the New Testament came to be in its present form.

It is noteworthy that although not one of the *original* manuscripts exists today, more evidence exists for the validity of the New Testament copies than for the validity of any other ancient piece of literature, including the works of Caesar, Plato, and Aristotle. When the King James Version was written in the early 1600s, the translators used the oldest known *copies* of the New Testament that they thought were credible. These copies were from the tenth century. But by the time the Revised Standard Version (RSV) was written, fourth-century copies of the Greek Bible had been found. These older copies were used to translate the RSV. But the miracle is that between the two translations there is 99.9 percent consistency, and in no place is there controversy on doctrine.

Even if these early copies had not been found, writings of the Church Fathers of the second and third centuries quote all but eleven verses of the entire New Testament. The existence of their writings today is a miracle of survival in itself.

While the Bible has been burned, destroyed, and ridiculed through the ages, it still remains the most sought-after book in the world. God not only inspired His Word within the writers, but He has kept His hand upon this Word throughout the centuries. While man will wither as the grass of the field, the Word of God will prevail forever (1 Pet. 1:24-25).

5. *Copies of the Bible*

So often we hear someone say that since no original Bible book exists, only copies (as is the case with all ancient books, due to the deterioration of scrolls), we have a distorted Bible today, filled with errors and ideas inserted by the copiers. First, we must remember that each new translation today is written from the oldest known sources, not a recent copy. Even so, every "new find" made by archaeologists is virtually identical to manuscripts found earlier. To date, the oldest Hebrew manuscripts of the Old Testament date back to the eighth century after Christ, except for fragments and excerpts such as those found in the caves above the Dead Sea in the late 1940s. The oldest Greek copies of the New Testament (Vatican and Sinaitic) date to the fourth century after Christ. We also have possession of Greek manuscripts of the Old Testament (copies of the Septuagint) that date back to the fourth century. Bible translations today are made from these ancient manuscripts, with careful reference also to hundreds of manuscript fragments that are even older than the complete copies.

Since the Bible can only be translated from copies of the original books, one naturally might ask, "How accurate are these copies?" Read this excerpt from Sidney Collett's *All About the Bible* (pp. 14-15).

In making copies of Hebrew manuscripts, which are the precious heritage of the church today, the Jewish scribes exercised the greatest possible care, even to the point of superstition—counting, not only the words, but every letter, noting how many times each particular letter occurred, and destroying at once the sheet on which a mistake was detected, in their anxiety to avoid the introduction of the least error into the sacred Scriptures, which they prized so highly and held in reverent awe. Moreover, each new copy had to be made from an approved manuscript, written with a special kind of ink, upon sheets made from the skin of a "clean" animal. The writers also had to pronounce aloud each word before writing it, and on no account was a single word to be written from memory. They were to reverently wipe their pen before writing the name of God in any form, and to wash their whole body before writing "Jehovah," lest that holy name should be tainted even in the writing. The new copy was then carefully examined with the original almost immediately; and it is said that if only one incorrect letter were discovered the whole copy was rejected!

Modern translations themselves are often looked at suspiciously. Why don't we use just the King James Version?

The English language has changed since the King James Version was completed in 1611. Newer translations seek to give a more understandable meaning of the Greek and Hebrew words of the Bible.

For example, the KJV, in over 300 places, uses seventeenth-century words whose meanings have since changed. KJV scholars used "let" where today we use "restrains" (see 2 Thess. 2:7). These words today are opposites. The KJV also reads "prevent" for "precede," "comprehend" for "overcome," "allege" for "prove," and "demand" for "ask." The word in the Greek text which means "immediately" is translated in some places in the KJV as "by and by." This does not make the KJV erroneous. It was written for the seventeenth-century Englishman, and to him then it was quite accurate. But our language has changed, so we must continually update older literature if we wish to perpetuate the original message.

Other words have become archaic. People no longer say: thou, thee, must needs, thy, doest, or walketh. This language is beautiful, but it is not common and it confuses a lot of Christians today.

In summary, let us remember that for hundreds of years men have been finding older manuscripts and digging into richer, more meaningful archaeological findings. And in every case we find that the Bible, as we have it today, is miraculously accurate, not only in the stories it tells but in its current, translated form. It reminds us of the Irishman who built his three-foot wall four feet wide so that if a storm blew it over it would be taller afterwards than before. The Bible keeps getting taller and stronger not weaker and more watered down.

In view of the many translations of the Bible available today, one might ask, "Which version of the Bible should we read?" No intention is made here to evaluate all of the many translations available. But the following guide may help.

1. To the everyday layman who trusts his pastor to direct him in doctrine but who wants to read the

Bible just to get the stories, a paraphrase such as *The Living Bible* reads very easily.

2. To the Christian who also trusts his pastor, but wants to study God's Word more closely himself, a parallel version of the Bible is recommended. A parallel version shows, side by side, four translations of the Bible. Thus the reader can compare four different translations of any particular verse.

3. If you want to memorize Scripture, use the KJV. It has become a standard for memorization, and its language is eloquent.

4. If you want to get "picky" with words or sentences to help you more soundly understand doctrine without being a famous scholar, buy a Greek-English Interlinear Translation of the New Testament. In this version you will be given a word-for-word translation from the oldest Greek into English. Along with this you will need a New Testament Greek dictionary to look up the Greek words and receive a more expanded, English definition.

Here is a brief overview of the more popular versions of the Bible used by Christians today.

The King James Version. The standard pulpit Bible, most common for memorization and quotation, possessing an angelic ring and rhythmic cadence admired by many. Published in 1611.

The Revised Standard Version. A revision of the 1901 American Standard Version, which was an updated revision of the King James Version. The RSV was made by thirty-two scholars. The New Testament was published in 1946, the Old Testament in 1952. An excellent version for study and ease of reading.

The Amplified Bible. In 1958, twelve California editors

produced this text giving alternative, expanded phrases suggesting different possible meanings. Good study Bible.

J.B. Phillips, The New Testament in Modern English. A fresh, easy-to-read paraphrase of the New Testament, written in 1958 and revised in 1972.

The New English Bible. A team of biblical scholars in 1961 and 1970 sponsored by British Bible societies and churches gave us this translation utilizing recent historical, linguistic and textual discoveries.

The Jerusalem Bible. The Roman Catholic School of Biblical Studies in 1966 produced this accurate and scholarly translation.

Today's English Version. Produced by the American Bible Society in 1966, a straightforward translation in everyday English.

The Living Bible (by Kenneth Taylor). A conservative paraphrase written in colloquial language for assisting the ordinary reader in understanding the Bible.

6. *How the Bible Has Affected Man*

No human being living in our civilized world has ever gone unaffected by God's book, the Bible. It has given us our calendar and the two greatest holiday celebrations of all, Christmas and Easter, marking the birth and resurrection of Jesus. Many of our children are given Bible names: James, Adam, Thomas, Samuel, Mary, John, Peter, Paul, Joseph, Elizabeth, Martha, Phillip, Stephen, Daniel, David, and Jonathan.

The teachings of God found in His Bible aroused men to abolish slavery. It has given dignity and equality to women, and it has given us the doctrine of marriage. The Bible inspired the concept of orphanages to replace the killing of unwanted children by the parents; it provided influence for the first home for the blind, the first hospital, and the first asylum. The first and greatest American schools were founded by the Christian church, inspired by the Bible: Brown University, Yale, Harvard, Princeton, William and Mary, the University of Pennsylvania, Dartmouth College.

History shows that nations of the past rose and fell according to their belief in the Bible. Note the heights of the Jews under Solomon, Rome under Constantine, England under Alfred the Great and Queen Elizabeth and Queen Victoria, and the United States under our Christian forefathers.

The world's greatest art and music (such as Michelangelo's *Pietà* and Handel's *Messiah*) were inspired by the Bible. Our doctrine of right and wrong, the morals of life, uses the Bible as a standard. The Bible has turned whole tribes of cannibals into missionaries. There is no other book in the world that changes so many skeptics into peace-filled believers, no other book that offers so much hope to the mentally disturbed, the physically ailing, the spiritually lost. Surely the Bible, this most amazing book, is God's word to man.

2

Noah's ark, Adam's Eden, Jonah's whale and other hard-to-swallow tales are easily tempered by today's "reasonable" society. Over a century of archaeological discoveries, however, give strong support to the Bible.

Noah's Ark and Other Hard-to-Swallow Tales

Archaeology relates to the Bible in two ways. First, archaeological discoveries support biblical statements thought to be in error. For example, Luke says Lysanias was tetrarch (ruler) of Abilene in A.D. 27 when John the Baptist was called to his ministry (Luke 3:1). However, according to history books, the only ruler with that name was a King Lysanias who was executed by the Roman General Marc Antony thirty years before John was born. Could Luke be wrong?

A Greek inscription carved in stone from a town near Damascus (the old Abilene territory) mentions one "Lysanias the Tetrarch" and contains the dates A.D. 14-29. This recent archaeological evidence proves Luke's facts to be accurate.

Second, archaeological discoveries fill in historical gaps not recorded in the Bible or in other history books.

A friend of Christianity
During the nineteenth century, liberals who produced so-called "higher criticism" joined with evolutionists to tear down the Bible shred by shred. With much specula-

tion, assumption, and concocted theories (guesses), they relied upon subjective data—the writings of men—as their base of opinion. Conservative Christians who clung to "biblical accuracy" became branded as ignorant; to be Christian was to be uneducated.

Thanks to the scientific objectivity of archaeology, which overrules the subjective basis of "higher criticism," Christianity is again becoming the religion of the educated. Pseudo-intellectuals who cling to the opinionated teachings of the past century are fading into the shadow of ignorance.

Many of our history books, which once seemed to contradict the biblical record, are now being reconstructed according to more recent archaeological finds. That archaeology has proven to be a friend and not a foe of Christianity is an established fact. While every biblical statement has not been vindicated by archaeology, none has ever been contradicted. So many historical facts of the Bible, displaying minute details, have been supported that the pattern of biblical accuracy has been established.

Recent Finds

For many years the scientific community of the past claimed that several of the biblical books were actually written years later than the incidents recorded, and contained inconsistencies in their historical facts. Supposedly, an "enlightened" look at the writings themselves would expose the Bibles "hoax."

For instance, the use of the word "brass" ("bronze" in the RSV, both an alloy of copper) in Exod. 38:8 was thought to be an inaccurate statement made by a writer much later than the 1491 B.C. setting of Exodus, for scholars thought bronze was not in use in the Middle East during the time of the Exodus. However, archaeological discoveries have shown a bronze age did exist between the prehistoric stone age and the iron age of 1000 B.C.*

In I Kings 7:16 there is mention of Solomon's casting metals. Metallurgy was considered of a later period, and this account was cited as "proof" of a hoax. However, archaeological excavations of Ezion-geber on the Red Sea in 1940 revealed a large smelting plant complete with complicated wind-harnessing air channels and flues in operation during this period. Here copper was refined and used in the construction of Solomon's temple.

Historically, there has been little evidence that the story of Joseph in Egypt was for real. The Bible has been the only source of this event. There is a reason for this.

Egypt always kept faithful records of their history, as far back as 3000 B.C. However, around 1730 B.C., the Hyksos, Semitic tribes from Canaan and Syria, stormed Egypt and set up their kingdom. Record keeping ceased. It was during this period that Joseph and the sojourn of the children of Israel into Egypt took place. Without historical records we must resort to indirect proof that the sojourn existed. The details of the biblical account are known to be typical of the day: Potiphar, to whom Joseph was sold, was a common Egyptian name (Gen. 37:36). Joseph's rise to viceroy of Egypt as described in Gen. 41:42 is the exact protocol according to Eyptian reliefs and murals. The mention that Joseph rode in the Pharoah's "second chariot" (Gen. 41:43) seems to verify the period, for the Hyksos were the first to use the horse-drawn chariot in Egypt. And the titles used in the biblical account, "the chief of the butlers" and "chief

---

*The use of the word "steel" (a contemporary alloy) in 2 Sam. 22:35 is a poor translation made by the King James translators and should read "bronze," as in RSV.

of the bakers" (40:2), "overseer over his house" (39:4), "father to Pharaoh" (45:8) are known to be typical Egyptian titles. Also an ancient papyrus in the Brooklyn Museum lists seventy-nine slaves of an Egyptian household; forty of these names are Semitic. These observations give credibility to the story of Joseph and the children of Israel in Egypt.

Surely the writer of the story of Abraham exposed the "true" date of his writing when he wrote of camels in Egypt and travel from Mesopotamia to the Mediterranean—unheard of until the archaeologists' spade ascertained that camels were used in Egypt long before Abraham and that such travel was common in Abraham's day. Again archaeology verified the Bible.

Just a hundred years ago "higher critics," such as the influential Julius Wellhousen, held that Abraham was a wandering nomad of an ignorant and primitive nature, unfamiliar with geography, law, commerce, and history, and that the Genesis account was distorted by a more recent author. This account was largely supported by the fact that no one could produce any evidence of an Ur of Chaldees.

However, archeologists who have recently discovered Abraham's ancient city of Ur (2000 B.C.) say it was a highly advanced city complete with a library of clay tablets equivalent to math books, hymn books, receipts for business transactions, and even payrolls for female employees. Abraham was a man from a city of great culture. For him to leave with all of his house and animals to venture to a wilderness in an unknown land surely must have been an act of faith, as the Bible claims.

Likewise it was once believed that the complexity of the Levitical laws of 1500 B.C. was too great for the primitive nature of that era, falsifying the biblical accounts. Archaeological discoveries of the clay tablets of Ras Shamra reveal similar complex laws that existed even before the period of the Levitical laws.

In the fifth chapter of Daniel we read of the Babylonian King Belshazzar, who was killed when his country was overthrown by the Medo-Persians. Secular historians have never mentioned such a king and claimed the last king of Babylon was Nabonidus and that he was absent during the invasion. For many years the "intelligent" world chose to accept the incomplete writings of the secular historians and held the Bible in error.

In 1853 a cylinder was dug from the Euphrates Valley whose inscription revealed that indeed Nabonidus was king, but he had made his son, one *Belshazzar*, coruler (and upon his absence, ruler in charge). This double rule is brought to light in the Bible when Belshazzar announces that whoever can interpret the hand writing on the wall "shall be the *third* ruler in the kingdom" (Dan. 5:7).

Also held by liberal scholars quick to dilute the Bible was the non-existence of the Hittites. The Bible mentions them forty times, but secular historians knew nothing of their existence. Again the Bible was accused of error. In 1906 the Hittite capital, Boghazkoy, was unearthed along with thousands of Hittite texts including the Hittite code. Today, study of Hittite culture and language is taught in universities.

The grandeur and expanse of Solomon's wealth as mentioned in the Bible has always been suspect to "latter day scholars." That he had a navy (I Kings 9:26), 1400 chariots and 12,000 horsemen (10:26), and fortified several cities (9:15) was considered doubtful. But archaeological discoveries in the ancient city of Megiddo near Mt. Carmel in the 1930s revealed stalls for 400 horses in that city alone, a water trough with a capacity of 2,775 gallons, barracks for the chariot battalions, and a paved street from the enormous stable area to the city.

Human conversion is one of the great witnesses to the divine inspiration of the Bible, and archaeology, like any other profession, has its share. In the late 1800s a young English scholar named William Ramsey, acting upon the claims of his professors, began archaeological digs in Turkey and Greece for the sole purpose of refuting the stories of Jesus and the start of the early church as found in Luke and Acts. Dig after dig was made to relocate boundaries and prove that cities claimed to exist never actually existed and that the early stories were primarily fictitious.

With each new discovery the support for Luke's accuracy and detail piled high, until the brilliant researcher buckled to his knees and gave his heart (and his intelligent head) to the Lord. Sir William Ramsey became a Christian and a great Bible scholar. His writings today are still considered classics in the study of New Testament history.

In recent years there have been over 100 major discoveries that substantiate the biblical record. These include evidence in 1961 that Pontius Pilate was in fact high commissioner of Judea from A.D. 26 to A.D. 36, the discovery of the Pool of Bethesda where Jesus healed a lame man (John 5:2-15), in the 1950s the digging up of Jericho, and in 1961 the uncovering of the ancient south wall of Jerusalem.

Archaeology's support of the Bible is a remarkable fulfillment of a prophecy Jesus made as He rode into Jerusalem on a donkey many years ago. On Palm Sunday as He rode into the great city, shouts came forth, "Blessed be the King." The Pharisees asked Jesus to rebuke the crowd and stop the shouts. Jesus said, "If these should hold their peace, the stones would immediately cry out" (Luke 19:40).

Today, while many are trying to stop the shout of Christianity's uniqueness, the stones under the archaeologists' spades are crying out indeed.

Noah's Flood

Perhaps the greatest archaeological discoveries of our time are those which relate to the most mythical-sounding story in the Bible—Noah and the flood.

In Genesis, chapters 6-9, we are told of God's decision to destroy the inhabitants of earth because He "saw that the wickedness of man was great in the earth, and that every imagination of the thoughts of his heart was only evil continually" (6:5). He chose to destroy the inhabitants with a great deluge of water that not only poured from the sky as torrential rains but inundated the land from the deeps of the ocean.

> The same day were all the fountains of the great deep broken up, and the windows of heaven were opened. And the rain was upon the earth forty days and forty nights. (Gen. 7:11-12)

Archaeological discoveries of records of numerous races all over the world give accounts of this flood.

Traditions in Africa tell of a punishing deluge, a saving ark, and four rainbows.

In the Zend-Avesta, ancient Persia's sacred book, we find the story of Ahura Mazda, creator of the universe, who warns the king of a flood and instructs him to build an underground fortress of certain dimensions and fill it with a variety of animals.

In the record of a Hindu writing dated to the sixth century B.C. we find a myth about Manu, who is warned by a fish of an imminent deluge and advised to build a boat into which he is to take seven wise men and seeds of all species. Numerous versions of this particular story have been found.

A Chinese tradition tells of a gigantic flood that occurred in 2297 B.C. The only ones to escape were Fah-Le, his wife, and their three children.

In Latin and Greek mythology there are several accounts of a deluge. In one, Zeus was to flood the earth. Deucalion, the king, is warned by Prometheus to build a large chest. After floating on the waters of destruction for nine days and nine nights, the king and his wife emerge and repopulate the earth by throwing stones over their shoulders. The king's stones became men, his wife's stones women. Other legends and myths occur from Icelandic, Welsh, and Lithuanian traditions.

In the Pacific Islands in Melanesia, in Samoa, in New Britain, and in Australia there are legends of a flood that have enough originality to exclude them from any influence of the biblical account.

Likewise, in South America there are several Indian legends of a great flood caused by a volcanic eruption and an earthquake. The inhabitants of Chile gathered supplies and climbed high in the mountains. The Peruvian account says a llama warned its master of the coming flood.

In Central America, an Aztec tale discloses a flood that destroys all of mankind except one man and woman, who float in a boat above the waters to a high mountain.

The Alaskan Eskimo legend tells of a flood and

earthquake from which the survivors escape by canoe.

The American Indian version tells of a lake that overflows to inundate the earth. The lone survivor remolds the land from a handful of clay and restores plant life by shooting arrows into trees.

Perhaps the most interesting account of the flood is related on a cuneiform tablet discovered in Nineveh, dated the seventh century B.C. It is called *The Gilgamesh Epic* and tells how God commanded a man to build a ship 120 cubits square and cover it with bitumen, the same pitch used by Noah to seal his ark. When the man and his family and many creatures entered the ship, a great flood came and covered the mountains. As the waters abated, a dove and a raven were sent to find dry land.

Accounts of a great flood appear in records of over thirty ancient races all over the world. Each tells of water that destroys a former civilization, some type of an ark of safety, one or more people who are preserved to establish a new civilization, and the salvaging of animal species. In each there is a Noahlike hero and, in most, a god or gods were pleased. Some are farfetched, but all give a definite account of a worldwide, disastrous flood. While some of these accounts, such as *The Gilgamesh Epic*, are close distortions of the biblical account, many are so unique in nature and geographically removed from the biblical writers that they become extrabiblical records of a worldwide flood in our not-too-distant past.

Waters from Below

Many today think of the flood as simply a forty-day rainstorm since they have not read closely that the "fountains of the great deep" also flooded the earth. One speculative explanation for these "fountains" is that heavenly bodies drifting close to the earth during that period of history caused the ocean tides to be displaced enough to flood the world as they moved across the earth in enormous waves.

Another theory says subterranean upheavals in the earth's crust caused mountains in the ocean floors to swell several thousand feet, displacing billions of tons of water, which covered the earth in gigantic tidal waves. Verification of these theories is perhaps evident from the many archaeological discoveries of seashells and marine life fossils found in inland mountains around the world. Deep pock marks over the entire earth's surface also unmistakenly witness to a cataclysmic flood of great proportions.

In 1929, diggings near Ur of Chaldees north of the Persian Gulf revealed a layer of water-deposited clay eight feet deep. There is indeed geological and archaeological evidence of the flood all over the world.

The notion that the events of the flood lasted only forty days is not accurate. A careful study of the Bible shows that to build an ark the dimensions of Noah's would have taken many months, perhaps years. Noah entered the ark seven days before the flood began (Gen. 7:10). The waters began to pour on the seventeenth day of the second month of Noah's six-hundredth year on earth (7:11). After many weeks of rainfall, many months of prevailing and abating waters, and several additional weeks of testing for dry land, Noah and his family left the ark. The Bible says Noah left the ark on the twenty-seventh day of the second month of his six-hundred-and-first year (8:13-14). Thus we see that Noah and his family were in the ark one year and seventeen days.

Evidence of a catastrophic, worldwide flood is abundant,

but if the story of Noah and the ark is not just another myth, where then is the ark? Explorers have documented evidence that it still rests near the summit of Mt. Ararat close to the border of Russia, Turkey, and Iran, embedded in ice right where Noah left it (8:4).

Noah's Ark

The earliest account known today of an ark on Mt. Ararat is that of a Babylonian priest, Berose, who wrote of the history of Chaldea several hundred years before Christ. Berose wrote that people continue to ascend Mt. Ararat and break small chunks of pitch from the ark to use as talismans.

The historian Josephus, who was alive when Jesus went to the cross, wrote in his *Antiquities of the Jews* that the remains of the ark on Ararat are still shown by the Armenians.

In 1840, the Turkish government sent teams of workers up Ararat to build fortifications against avalanches. One team discovered the front of a very old wooden ship jutting from a frozen glacier. If this was not Noah's ark, what then would have lifted a ship of this size to the peak of a large mountain whose top has been embedded in snow and ice for centuries?

James Bryce of the British Parliament scaled Mt. Ararat in 1876. Few explorers have ever reached its icy peaks. At an altitude of 16,400 feet he saw a hand-hewn piece of wood about four feet long and five inches thick jutting from a block of volcanic lava.

Mt. Ararat is a volcanic group, and researchers claim that due to eruptions and glacial movement, the ark has probably shifted locations and perhaps been broken.

Other climbers and avalanche research teams from

Turkey claimed to have seen portions of the ark embedded under a glacier with its end protruding. One expedition reported compartments or rooms inside the ark with ceilings fifteen feet high.

In 1916, a Russian pilot named Roskovitsky spotted the skeleton of a huge ship the size of a city block while flying over the eastern side of the snow-capped mountain. A Russian expedition of scientists and 150 workers returned and climbed the mountain, found the wreck, took pictures and delivered wood samples to Petrograd. During the Russian revolution the following year all documents disappeared. Twenty-five years later, another Russian pilot and expedition verified the earlier discovery.

Because of the Ararat area being a military zone, permission to freely explore has not come easily to would-be explorers. Perhaps the greatest discovery of our day is from the expeditions of a French industrialist, Fernand Navarra, described in his book *Noah's Ark: I Touched It* (Logos, 1974).

His first expedition in 1952 brought him and his team through much struggle against the competing elements of steep inclines, frequent landslides, thin air, freezing winds, and icy slopes to conquer the summit nearly 17,000 feet above sea level.

But more important, at a lower elevation and on the west side, Navarra, while standing alone on a large cap of ice saw below him a large, dark mass approximately 120 yards long. Navarra had located the ark but lacked the necessary equipment to approach it during this trip.

After failing to reach the site during a second expedition in 1953, Navarra and his eleven-year-old son, Raphael, returned in 1955. During this trip, they succeeded in reaching the site of the ark. Crossing a treacherous, crevice-riddled glacier, and waiting out an all-night blizzard that complicated the terrain with thirteen inches of snow, Navarra descended forty feet into a deep crevasse by rope ladder and came upon the ark embedded in ice below the gigantic glacier. He chopped off a heavy, five-foot, hand-hewn beam, which was hauled up by his son standing on a narrow ridge on the surface of the glacial ice pack. The beam was photographed, chopped into smaller pieces, and smuggled off the mountain as fire wood.

Navarra received many offers to return to Mt. Ararat but did not until he led a team of Americans in 1968. The site was found, but thick snow and a lack of time prohibited further exploration.

Back in the states the SEARCH Foundation was created, and in 1969 they returned. Forced to use different search techniques due to changes in the ice pack since 1955, only a half dozen small pieces of the same wood was discovered. But this time it was by an organized, professional research team operating under permit.

The wood from Navarra's 1955 discovery has been tested by several scientific laboratories, including the National Museum of Natural History, Comparative Anatomy of Living Plants and Fossils in Paris, France; Forestry Institute of Research and Experiments in Madrid, Spain; The University of Bordeaux, Department of Anthropology and Prehistoric Studies in Bordeaux, France; and the Center for Forestry Research and Analysis in Paris, France.

The conclusions of these laboratories is that the wood is oak, it was hand-hewn, and is about 5000 years old, the approximate date of Noah's ark.

The importance of the discovery of Noah's ark must not be overlooked. If it is proven that Noah's ark rests upon Mt. Ararat, then it is proven that the greatest alleged "myth" of the Bible is no myth at all, but fact. If the *greatest* "myth" is proven fact, then it is more likely that the yet unproven *smaller* "myths" are factual also.

Other Extravagant Bible Stories

One such story is that of Adam and Eve. No one has been able to prove that a real Garden of Eden existed, because no Eden has been found. Opponents of the Bible say the story of the Garden is a product of earlier man's imagination in an attempt to explain the derivation of man.

The discovery of the ruins of a Garden of Eden are unlikely, because no civilization, craftsmen, or builders ever lived there. Gen. 2:10-14 says a river went out of Eden and parted into four rivers. Two of these are known today, the Euphrates and the Tigris (RSV). The other two are unknown. Near Bagdad, Iraq, the Euphrates and Tigris come close together. One theory says these two rivers could have joined together here to become the site of Eden before the flood. Therefore Eden would have had two rivers coming in and two rivers departing and each could have been given a name, thus four rivers.

But we must remember there was a flood, a very large one that would have destroyed Eden and changed the face of the earth and possibly the existence and direction of rivers. As to the whereabouts of the Garden of Eden we must again be content with the words of Moses:

> The secret things belong unto the Lord our God: but those things which are revealed belong unto us and to our children for ever, that we may do the words of

28

this law. (Deut. 29:29)

Another alleged "tale" is that of Jonah, who was swallowed by a whale. Whale-of-a-tale as this seems, there is nothing in the biblical account that appears unreal.

To begin with, the Bible never says a "whale" swallowed Jonah. The Old Testament account in Jon. 1:17 says it was a "great fish." In the New Testament in Matt. 12:40 the translation reads "whale" but should read "sea monster," a better translation of the Greek rendering.

But whether it was a whale or not is immaterial, because whales do exist that can easily swallow men whole.

The humpback whale, a toothless type that swallows its food whole, grows to an easy fifty feet in length. The sulfur-bottom whale grows to seventy-five feet and longer. Certain baleen whales, weighing over 300,000 pounds, measure up to 100 feet long.

The April 4, 1896, issue of *Literary Digest* gives the account of a Mediterranean whale that swallowed a harpoonist, after destroying his boat. A day and a half later the man was found alive in the dead whale's stomach. The sailor's name was James Bartley, and he suffered only from gastric juice burn.

The whale is actually a mammal and stores a vast amount of breathable air in a nasal chamber that measures seven by seven by fourteen feet in the larger species. If a whale imbibes an object it desires not to swallow, the object is thrust into the air chamber and ejected when the whale surfaces. Also, if a whale becomes ill, it will eject the contents of its large and many-chambered stomach.

Besides whales, there are several sharks that are capable of swallowing a man, and even whole horses have been found inside their stomachs. The whale shark averages fifty feet in length and, having no teeth, strains its food through large plates in its mouth.

Archaeology can't prove Jonah was indeed swallowed by a fish or whale, but marine biologists today verify the possibility of such a case.

The Bible is abundant with great miracles of God that are prime targets to attack with "reason." Such miracles include the Tower of Babel and the confounding of tongues (Genesis 11), Joshua commanding the sun to halt (Josh. 10:12), the fiery destruction of Sodom and Gomorrah (Genesis 19), and the turning of Lot's wife to a pillar of salt (Gen. 19:26). Yet God, in giving us His Bible, is not attempting to "prove" each statement. He is only telling us the way it was and is.

3

Is our New Testament incomplete today? Whatever happened to the Gospel of Thomas, Third Corinthians and the Acts of James? What became of . . .

The Lost Books of the Bible

All the books of the New Testament were written between the cross (A.D. 30) and the end of the first century. During the following 100 years, however, numerous letters, acts, gospels and apocalypses (revelations) were written. Because most of these books are now lost, many have termed them the "lost books of the Bible." The real truth to their disappearance is that the early church, recognizing their erroneous nature, lack of inspiration, contradictions, and geographical and chronological errors, did not keep these writings with the inspired writings they had collected. And so, they eventually disappeared, like other unimportant writings of the day.

The New Testament books were written during the first century by men who knew Christ or were closely related to Him. The "lost books" were written a hundred years later by men who were trying to expand on God's word already written. Today they are called *apocryphal New Testament*, books because they are of the Christian era and because they are "hidden" (apocryphal means of doubtful origin, or lost).

Do not confuse the *apocryphal New Testament* books with the *Apocrypha*, a collection of fourteen books sometimes found between the Old and the New Testament.

These latter historical and religious writings also contain many geographical and chronological errors and were rejected by the Council of Laodicea in A.D. 363 as being uninspired writings.

The apocryphal New Testament books (actually letters and stories) were a part of the early Christian church. For the first hundred years or more the forming church had literature that has since proven itself untrustworthy. It wasn't until about 150 years after Pentecost that the church in Rome listed twenty-two books as their New Testament. Most of these exist in our Bible today, with the exception of *The Letter of Barnabas* and *The Shepherd of Hermas.* It is doubtful that these two books or any other "lost book" preserve any significant unrecorded traditions, actions, or words of Jesus, or his followers, not already recorded.

Some of these books are still available today, while many are lost completely. Those lost are known by references made to them and even short quotes found in other books. Some scholars have suggested that of those that are lost a few (such as the *Gospel of the Hebrews* and the *Gospel of the Egyptians*) if found would be superior to the canonical books (those in the Bible today). This speculation is doubtful.

For the most part, these last books are expansions of the books found in today's Bible. With the expansions come erroneous developments of themes. For example, in the *Acts of Thomas* we read that Mary was brought up in the temple, an expansion of Samuel's upbringing. This theme expansion is characteristic of most of the apocryphal Acts. Historical significance of these books is denied only when their assertions are contrary to the books of the canon; if canonical data is claimed to be erroneous, historical significance of the apocryphal books becomes suspect.

This statement should not imply that these books are without value. In many places they support or amplify issues presented in the canon. They also reveal the hopes and attitudes of Christians in the early church. Of profound importance is the fact that they offer evidence that no reliable gospel was written before Mark's gospel some thirty-five years after the resurrection. This realization implies incidents recorded in all other gospels or biographies of Jesus are expansions of Mark's Gospel. That these biographies existed in A.D. 75 or 80 when Luke, a Greek physician, researched his Gospel is evident in the opening statement of Luke, "Several biographies of Christ have already been written. . . . However it occurred to me that it would be well to recheck all these accounts . . . and . . . pass this summary on to you" (Luke 1:1, TLB).

Infancy Gospels

Many of the apocryphal gospels are known only from an occasional quotation. Others fall into two categories, those referring to the hidden years before Jesus' ministry (these are purely imaginary) and those of events after the crucifixion. In the first category, the *Protevangelium of James* gives a legendary account of the birth and rearing of the Virgin Mary, and the *Gospel of Thomas* discloses miracles wrought by Jesus as a small boy. Both are unsupported by the canon. All other infancy gospels are expansions of these two.

Passion Gospels

The second group is called the passion gospels. Here we have fragments of the *Gospel of Peter* found in an

Egyptian tomb in 1886, the *Acts of Pilate* (sometimes called the *Gospel of Nicodemus*), and the *Gospel of Bartholomew*, which lists a series of questions asked of Jesus after His resurrection.

The *Gospel of Peter* was supposed to have been written by Peter. Along with the *Book of James* it indicates that the brothers of Jesus were the sons of Joseph by a previous marriage. This book lays all blame of the crucifixion upon the Jews and quotes Jesus' last words on the cross as, "My power, my power, thou hast forsaken me," instead of, "My God, my God, why hast thou forsaken me?" as recorded in Matt. 27:46. That the Matthew record is correct and the apocryphal record spurious is evident when we read Psalm 22, a prophetic utterance of King David recorded a thousand years before Jesus' birth. Its opening statement is, "My God, my God, why hast thou forsaken me?"

Although no events in the *Gospel of Peter* are contradictory to the canon, the authorship of the book appears to be spurious. For example, one statement begins, "But I, Simon Peter, and Andrew my brother, took our nets . . ." However, evidence has shown this book to have been written around A.D. 150, which, of course, is about eighty-five years after Peter was crucified (upside down at his own request) in Rome under Nero. Books allegedly written by one person and whose real author is unknown are called pseudepigrapha. Many of the "lost books" are pseudepigraphic.

The *Acts of Pilate* (or *Gospel of Nicodemus*) was probably written late in the fourth century. It gives an account of the trials of Jesus before Pilate and the Sanhedrin's proof of His resurrection and ascension. Pilate is shown giving great reverence to Jesus. Twelve witnesses bear testimony that Joseph and Mary were married and that Jesus was not born out of fornication. Three other witnesses, a priest, a rabbi, and a Levite testify to seeing Christ ascend on the mountaintop. Part two of this book is the testimony of two men brought back from Hades when Christ went to set the spirits free. They relate the whole account of their death, the underworld, Satan, Christ's arrival, and so forth. Although the *Acts of Pilate* is written in the first person ("I Pilate"), Pilate died over 200 years before the book was written.

Besides the five mentioned, additional gospels of the early Christian era include: *Arabic Gospel of the Infancy, Gospel of Basilides, Gospel of Ebronites, Gospel of the Birth of Mary, Gospel of the Nazarenes, Gospel of Philip,* and others.

Acts

The apocryphal Acts contain a series of five romances, usually ending with the martyrdom of the apostle. These are all authored by Leucius around A.D. 150, according to fifth-century beliefs. The books are: *Acts of John, Acts of Paul, Acts of Peter, Acts of Thomas* and *Acts of Andrew.*

The *Acts of John* is a succession of stories, miracles, and discourses of John in Asia Minor. Only about one-third of the book is still available. On one account it testifies that John prayed away a swarm of bedbugs from a deserted inn. The account of John's death finds him digging a grave into which he throws his clothes and then sprawls. Herein he thanks God for keeping his body "untouched by union with a woman," then gives up the ghost. The stories all reveal hostility to marriage and sex.

The *Acts of Paul* contain an account of Paul's preaching on chastity. The sermon is overheard by Thecla, a Greek girl of prominent background. Thecla breaks her marriage engagement, visits Paul in prison, becomes a missionary, and baptizes herself in a pool of seals. She becomes a famous virgin martyr. The *Acts of Paul* also give a description of Paul as, "a man of stature, thin-haired upon the head, crooked in the legs, of good state of body, with eyebrows joining, and nose somewhat hooked." There is also mention of Paul baptizing a lion.

The *Acts of Peter* reveal a dog speaking. But we must remember that the supernatural is natural in the hands of God, for in Num. 22:28, He causes an ass to speak. The *Acts of Peter* also gives the account of Peter's crucifixion in Rome, and mentions a dry sardine that was made to swim again.

The *Acts of Thomas* is the only one of its sort to still exist in complete form today. It relates events in the life of Thomas. One episode is of a serpent who has jealously slain a woman's lover. The serpent confesses this and all other evil deeds since the Garden of Eden then dies. Many animals speak in this gospel. Another episode relates the story of a dragon punished for squirting poison on an enemy.

The *Acts of Andrew* was probably the last penned by Leucius. It accounts for the life and martyrdom of Andrew. Most of the tales appear to have been edited.

Other apocryphal Acts include: *Acts of Andrew and Paul, Acts of Barnabas, Ascents of James, Passion (martyrdom) of Paul, Preaching of Peter,* and *Acts of Thaddaeus.*

Epistles

A few of the early epistles are known, but they were

not as abundant as the other writings.

The *Epistle of the Apostles* is a second-century statement of beliefs and expectations in letter form by the eleven apostles. This letter, now in its entire form in Ethiopic, summarizes a revelation to the Apostles by Jesus after His resurrection. Other epistles include: The *Third Epistle to the Corinthians* (a part of the *Acts of Paul*), *Epistle to the Laodiceans*, and *Epistle of Titus*.

Apocalypses

The fourth group of apocryphal writings is the apocalypses, accounts of several apostles' tours of heaven and hell.

The first and most famous is the *Apocalypse of Peter*. In early Bibles, it often followed the canonical book of Revelation. Clement of Alexandria regarded it as canonical. Today the *Apocalypse of Peter* still exists in its complete form. There are scenes of transfiguration and a description of some of the torments of hell. One such account shows men standing with fire below burning their feet. Adulterous women are hung by their hair. Dante, the thirteenth-century Italian poet, must have used much of this book in writing his *Inferno*. This apocalypse is probably earlier than the *Gospel of Peter*.

The *Apocalypse of Paul* is an expansion of the Bible's record of Paul's visit to third heaven in 2 Cor. 12:2. This book reveals the story of the discovery of the book in Paul's former home in Tarsus, the Lord's commands to Paul to preach, a lengthy account of the daily chores of angels, Paul's meeting with Enoch, a view of the throne showing David next in command after Christ, and Paul's tour of hell and the torments viewed there.

Other apocalypses include: *Apocalypse of James*,

37

Apocalypse of Steven, Apocalypse of Thomas, and *Apocalypse of the Virgin.*

In addition to these are several Gnostic apocalypses, including *Apocalypse of Dositheus, Wisdom of Jesus, Apocalypse of Messos, Acts of Peter and the twelve Apostles,* and *Dialogue of the Savior.*

Besides the four major divisions of apocryphal writings there exists a long list of related books such as, *Agrapha* (supposed collection of sayings of Jesus), *Apostolic Constitutions and Canons, Melkon, Pistis Sophia,* and the baffling *Books of Jeu.*

Why Rejected

The greatest single feature of all the "lost" books that caused their rejection from the canon is their lack of apostolic authorship. Only the earliest writings of those who knew Jesus or worked and toured with those who did (such as Luke) were accepted, and then only if they had qualities and evidence of divine inspiration. The books that were allowed to decay were erroneous and pseudepigraphic.

One of the great miracles of today is the fact that no group of leaders ever sat down and selected the canonical books. God himself through divine providence directed their emergence from amidst widely scattered churches.

Today we have twenty-seven New Testament and thirty-nine Old Testament books accepted by Christian churches as being of the canon. None of the apocryphal New Testament books have been accepted since the end of the second century.

4

Did you ever wonder why there seems to be so many sevens and forties in the Bible? Or whether or not those very large numbers found in some locations are for real? God uses numbers to help relay His message to man, but we must know . . .

How to Interpret Biblical Numbers

Biblical numbers should not be dismissed as superstitious insertions of an ancient race of people: The Bible is not simply a history book of Israel; it is God's message and revelation to the human race. Numbers used in the Bible are God-directed and used for good reason. Scholars often disagree as to how biblical numbers should be interpreted. Upon close examination it can be seen that numbers are used four different ways in the Bible: literally, poetically, mystically, and symbolically. Even in the presence of disagreement most scholars agree that numbers are important to the overall study of the Bible, especially in prophecy and in chronology. Here are the four ways numbers are used in the Bible.

Literal Numbers
The ancient Hebrews knew how to add, subtract, multiply, divide, and work with fractions. Evidence of all these functions are found in the Old Testament. They were also aware of the concepts of infinity (Gen. 13:16). Numbers used in a literal manner in the Bible display a remarkable degree of accuracy, even though modern math and exactness were not common until the time of the Greeks, long after the Old Testament was written.

The most common use of numbers in the Bible is the conventional or literal use, where 500 means 500 units of something. Literal biblical numbers are used both in the exact sense and as rounded-off approximations, as in the case of Gen. 26:12 and Matt. 19:29, where 100 is not meant to be taken exactly but as a close approximation, just as in the English language. Even numbers which appear exaggerated, however, such as the 7000 sheep of 2 Chron. 15:11 and the 30,000 chariots of 1 Sam. 13:5, after close scrutiny show literal intention. Such numbers were meant to be taken literally.

To use the number 40 as an example, we can find several references to its literal exact use; see Gen. 7:17 and 25:20. There are also examples of its literal rounded-off use, as in the case of Judg. 3:11, 5:31, and 8:28, where "and the land had rest for forty years" is considered by most scholars as an approximation.

Poetic Numbers

Sometimes the Bible uses numbers in a poetic or rhetorical sense; in these cases a literal interpretation should not be applied. Numbers used in this manner are intended to convey such concepts as "many" or "few."

A good example is found in Psalm 91, where we read, "A thousand may fall at your side, ten thousand at your right hand; but it will not come near you" (verse 7, RSV). And in 1 Sam. 18:7 we read, "Saul hath slain his thousands, and David his ten thousands."

Rhetorical numbers such as these must be interpreted poetically and not literally. Would you dare interpret literally the use of numbers in the very important statement found in Matt. 18:20, "For where two or three are gathered in my name, there am I in the midst of them" to imply that if four were gathered Jesus would not enter into their fellowship?

Mystical Numbers

Some students believe that since the Bible, like the universe, is a product of God, it too will exhibit numerical and symmetrical design. They seek hidden truths and special revelations by assigning numerical value to words and letters found in the Bible. This system of study was begun by the Greek philosopher/mathematician Pythagoras in the sixth century B.C. His followers developed a sort of number worship as their ideas spread from Greece into Italy and Judea, where their system provided the basis for Bible numerics. It is believed by some that Bible numerics can provide Christian growth for those who seek it, that the numbers can "prove scientifically" that the Bible is the inspiration of God, and that the original text of the Bible (none in existence today) can be reconstructed via Bible numerics. It is also believed that when the Bible passage reveals some aspect of the number seven, it is inspired. For example:

Consider Gen. 1:1, "In the beginning God created the heaven and the earth." In the Hebrew language there are seven words in this statement, which have fourteen syllables (two times seven) and twenty-eight letters (four times seven). Examples such as this are considered proof that the passage is divinely inspired and that it appears today as it did on the original scroll.

By assigning numerical values to letters, all the characters of the Bible become mystical numbers. One popularly analyzed passage is found in Rev. 13:18. Here the beast, or Antichrist, is assigned a numerical value of

666. Some have shown that Nero (in Hebrew) had a value of 666. Others have shown the founder of the Ku Klux Klan to have the number 666. Still others show recent and current world leaders, with their names numerically totaling 666, to be the Antichrist.

Most prominent Bible scholars consider mystical interpretations of biblical numbers to be an artificial analytical system devised to complicate the simplicity of the Word of God.

Symbolic Numbers

Like the typology of the Old Testament, symbolic numbers have a double meaning. For example, Moses literally freed the children of Israel from bondage and death in Egypt in a *symbolic* representation of Jesus setting free the children of God from bondage and death in the world. Just as his symbolic act was literal, the literal interpretation of a number should *not* be dropped when a number appears to have a symbolic meaning.

Symbolic numbers were used to a small degree by the Babylonians and Egyptians in 2000 B.C. (the time of Abraham). The New Testament books do not use symbolic numbers as freely as the Old Testament, except in the Revelation.

Here is a table of the most common symbolic numbers and their interpretation:

One—unity
Two—separation, contrast, or division
Three—divine approval, perfection
Four—earth, world, and space
Six—of man (short of divinity)
Seven—the attributes of God, perfection
Ten—divine completeness in time

Twelve—God's people or governmental rule
Forty—a test or trial
Seventy—God's ruling over the world.

Numerous passages in the Bible support these interpretations.

All scholars agree that seven employs strong symbolism in the Bible. Some feel it is the *only* number with symbolic connotations. Seven is found in almost 600 passages in the Bible. Often it illuminates a period of work and rest, such as with: God's creation in seven days (Gen. 2:2); Jacob's employment for seven years (Gen. 29:20); Joseph's seven years of plenty and seven years of famine (Gen. 41:53-54); Samson's seven-day marriage feast (Judg. 14:12); Jethro's seven daughters (Exod. 2:16); the seven lambs for burnt offering under the law (Num. 28:11); Naaman's dip in the Jordan seven times (2 Kings 5:10); and the seven rams, seven altars, and seven oxen of Balak (Num. 23:1).

We also find seven used frequently in the book of Revelation as God reveals future events to the Apostle John. We read of the seven churches (though there were more than that in Asia Minor) (1:4); seven spirits (1:4); seven candlesticks (1:12); seven stars (1:16); seven lamps (4:5); seven seals, horns, eyes, angels, trumpets, thunders— eighteen different sevens altogether. They symbolically represent God and verify that the revelation is divine.

Forty is another number that carries strong symbolic meaning. It appears often where a trial or testing period exists. The deluge of Noah's day lasted forty days; Moses spent forty years in Egypt; forty years in Midian, forty days on the mountain, fell before God forty days and nights, and spent forty years wandering in the wilderness with the children of Israel. Elijah was forty days enroute to Horeb, and Jonah warned Ninevah that the citizens had forty days in which to repent. Even in the life of Jesus, we find He fasted in the wilderness forty days; the length of His ministry was forty months; He made forty geographical journeys; and there were forty days between His resurrection and ascension. These literal events all portray the symbolic connotation of testing.

It is often difficult in biblical numerology to determine exactly how to interpret numbers. Most numbers, however, should simply be accepted literally, either as exact numbers or as approximations. Often Scriptures are rejected because their numbers seem unreal: God created the earth in "seven" days; the Israelites making their exodus out of Egypt numbered over "two million"; it rained for "forty days and forty nights"; the average age at death before the flood was "857 years old." In nearly every case, if you study Bible commentaries and ask God to guide you, you will find these numbers were meant to be taken literally.

Occasionally, numbers are used in a poetic sense where it is evident. Or symbolically if the number fits a truth-supporting pattern.

Mystical use of numbers is rare in the Bible. There is no evidence that words or letters were ever given mystical, numerical values.

We must remember the Bible is God's book. He selected the subjects, and the numbers, and inspired the writers to record them. It is most unrewarding to judge and dismiss as invalid any portion of God's word on the basis that the numbers seem unreal—or on any basis, for that matter.

5

Half of the books of the New Testament were written by one man—a powerful and talented man who spent half his life opposing the Christian belief. Surely his life qualifies as . . .

The Greatest Conversion in History

At about the same time Jesus lay in a manger in Bethlehem, another Hebrew child was born several hundred miles away in the town of Tarsus in what is now southern Turkey. His parents, while living outside of Palestine, chose to follow the ways of the Hebrews. Being of the tribe of Benjamin, they named their son Saul, after Israel's first king.

Youth and Education

Saul grew to love his home town. He was greatly influenced by the varied languages, merchandise, and customs seen at the wharves lining the river that passed through Tarsus and emptied into the Mediterranean a few miles away. There was much timber and thousands of goats kept on the neighboring hills. The long, fine goat's hair was woven into a coarse fabric and manufactured into numerous articles, including tents, which provided a trade for the young Saul. Tarsus was a capital city of great wealth, commerce, and learning. The university of Tarsus was equal to those of Athens and Alexandria. While Saul never attended the university, he certainly was exposed to its intellectual participants and the Stoic philosophy of "reasonable" thinking prominent in that day. Tarsus was also the center of a species of Baal-worship and idolatrous orgies of unimaginable sin.

It was here in Tarsus that Saul unknowingly was prepared to encounter men of every race and class and to look with sympathy and tolerance upon the most diverse customs and habits. Saul knew every form of man, and he learned logic in order to argue reasonably and convincingly. Saul, as a Hebrew, was qualified not only to be accepted by the Jews, but he had an extensive culture that provided acceptance in any society. He spoke many languages, and enjoyed the prestige of Roman citizenship (a prized inheritance won by his father). With this background Saul had the privilege of trial by Roman courts, with the right to appeal to Caesar, and he also exercised his religious rights as a Jew. Saul was well protected judicially, and to God this meant a potentially long missionary career. His career was in fact ten times the length of Jesus' brief ministry. Jesus lacked the judicial protection which clothed Saul.

Saul the Pharisee

About the time Jesus celebrated his twelfth birthday with a trip to Jerusalem, Saul too was sent to Jerusalem. Rather than follow in the trades as his father, he was to become a rabbi, a Pharisee. He entered the school at Jerusalem and studied under the most noted teacher the Jews have ever possessed, Gamaliel. Here Saul learned the Scriptures thoroughly and had his keen wit sharpened and his views enlarged. It was universally believed in that day that the promised Messiah would come only to a nation who kept the law *perfectly*—if even one person could keep the law perfectly. The law, however, included not only the ceremonial law of Moses but the hundreds of laws added by the Pharisees. This set of regulations was so vast it was impossible to keep the law "to the letter," but Saul became zealous to acquire this prize for his people.

It was with this frame of mind that Saul graduated, a scholar, and entered his teaching profession. Where he went to minister no one knows; perhaps back to Tarsus. But as the years intervened, Jesus' ministry stormed through Palestine. It was after the death and resurrection of Jesus that we find Saul returning to Jerusalem. There is conflict in his soul, for he has not been able to find peace and fellowship with God through his struggle with the law. Isn't there some work he can establish that will circumvent his deficiencies and win grace with God?

Christianity's Principal Opponent

In Jerusalem, Saul learns of the new, "blasphemous" sect which believes the crucified Jesus is the promised Messiah. Christianity was only two or three years old at that time and was confined primarily to Jerusalem. Gamaliel's influence had convinced the authorities that if they would ignore the Christians they would die out. But soon the new sect began to burst out of the old wine bags of Judaism, and Stephen rose to preach Christianity as freedom from the yoke of the law, the same law Saul had been trying to keep perfectly. As rage replaced logic in his Hebrew opponents, Stephen was stoned. At his execution we find officiating one Saul of Tarsus (Acts 7:58).

The zeal with which Saul struck back at the Christians brought him recognition and a promotion to membership in the Sanhedrin, the Jewish supreme court. To Saul was granted the authority to uproot the new sect of

Christianity. He had been striving so hard to please God; here was his chance in one splendid act of service to make up his deficiencies in keeping the law and to find peace with God.

Saul lashed out at the Christians. He stormed from house to house, dragging men and women off to prison and punishment. Like a madman he broke the church at Jerusalem, scattering the Christians far and wide (unintentionally helping the spread of the gospel, as "they that were scattered abroad went everywhere preaching the word").

Saul searched the cities of Palestine, then acquired from the high priest judiciary powers to seek out and imprison the Christians in the capital of Syria, Damascus.

On the Road to Damascus

His anger swelled during the six-day journey to Damascus. On the road just outside his destination at noon, when all but the most impatient travelers would have taken refuge from the intense heat with a long siesta, Saul pressed onward. News of his approach had already reached Damascus, and Christians there were in prayer. Their prayers were heard, and at midday, on the road to Damascus, Saul had a visitor. An intense light shone upon Saul's party, and all fell to the ground. A voice came from the presence of the light, "Saul, Saul, why persecutest thou me?" As Saul looked upon the radiant figure he asked, "Who art Thou, Lord?" And the answer came, "I am Jesus whom thou persecutest."

From this most dramatic of all Christian conversions (Acts 9), Saul rose and entered Damascus where for three days he was blind and did not eat. Though unable to see and without physical food, Saul was illuminated and filled from within.

God had selected Saul before he was even born (Gal. 1:15). God saw to it that he was well qualified culturally, politically, and religiously to become the great apostle to the Gentiles, to the Jews, and to kings (Acts 9:15). All of the zeal and thrust mustered by Saul over the years to keep the law crumbled to the earth, as Jesus lifted him in love and remolded him for the awaiting task.

Saul was a born thinker. This new, direction-changing truth which had been flashed upon him must now be worked into the structure of his convictions. Saul disappeared for three years into the wilderness of Arabia, probably the Sinai Peninsula where his ancestors had wandered with God for forty years. From there he emerged with new bearings and in full possession of his gospel. But there was to be another delay of seven or eight years. Waiting apparently is an instrument of discipline for those selected for exceptional work. During this period of preparation, the Gentiles were admitted to equal privileges with Jews in the forming church. The gospel became available to all.

The New Ministry

Almost simultaneously with the baptism of a Gentile family in Caesarea, a Gentile revival broke out in Antioch. It was here the doors opened for Saul to begin his great ministry, as he went to assist Barnabas.

For thirty years Saul traveled over 6000 miles in four missionary journeys, to establish the Christian church in over twenty cities in the Roman Empire, including Ephesus, Galatia, Corinth, Colosse, and Thessalonica. He spent half this time in prison, where he continued to praise the Lord. He was victorious over three ship-wrecks, a deadly snake bite, frequent lashings of thirty-nine strokes each, and he often was run out of town. But Saul's determination stood fast. It became obvious he had been cultivated by God in preparation to the fulfill-ing of his great missionary role.

Saul's tent-making ability provided funds for his jour-neys. He could speak all languages, relate to all men. He was most versatile. "I am made all things to all men, that I might by all means save some," he said (1 Cor. 9:22).

Saul had a renowned ability to write and speak well. His delivery was logical and understood by the simplest of men. He is credited with thirteen of the New Testa-ment letters, from Romans to Philemon, and is generally thought to be the author of Hebrews.

Saul was not one of the chosen twelve during Jesus' life on earth, but he came to be the greatest of them all, known today by the Roman rendering of his name, "Paul, called to be an apostle of Jesus Christ through the will of God" (1 Cor. 1:1).

The author of half the books of the New Testament—once a murderer of innocent people—stands as God's greatest picture of His grace toward men. Paul said:

How thankful I am to Christ Jesus our Lord for choosing me as one of his messengers . . . even though I used to scoff at the name of Christ. I hunted down his people, harming them in every way I could. . . . But God had mercy on me so that Christ Jesus could use me as an example to show everyone how patient he is even with the worst sinners, so others will realize that they, too, can have everlasting life. (1 Tim. 1:12-16, TLB)

PART TWO

THE UNIQUE MAN,
JESUS

6

How tall is Jesus? Does He have a beard, large eyes, long hair? The looks of Jesus remain a mystery. Yet there is biblical, historical, and archaeological evidence concerning . . .

What Jesus Looked Like

Jesus has a face. He is a human being. I say *is*, because He never lost His humanity, His appearance as a person. Jesus himself said, "Hereafter shall ye see the Son of man sitting on the right hand of power, and coming in the clouds of heaven" (Matt. 26:64). And Jesus *has* been seen as a man, after His death and resurrection. Stephen saw Him at the right hand of power. "But he, being full of the Holy Ghost, looked up stedfastly into heaven, and saw the glory of God, and Jesus standing on the right hand of God" (Acts 7:55).

In 1 John 4:2 we read, "Every spirit that confesseth that Jesus Christ is come in the flesh is of God." And after Jesus rose from the dead He stood before ten men and said, "Behold my hands and my feet, that it is I myself: handle me, and see; for a spirit hath not flesh and bones, as ye see me have" (Luke 24:39). Yes, the resurrected Jesus has flesh and bones, and He eats just as He did before His death on the cross. "And they gave him a piece of a broiled fish, and of an honeycomb. And he took it, and did eat before them" (Luke 24:42-43).

Indeed, Jesus is a human and has physical features. It is important that we remember this, because it is the very fact that Jesus is man that is the basis of our assurance that our sins are atoned and we are made whole through His sacrificial death. How else can Jesus identify with human sorrows and human suffering if He did not experience them with the same feelings as we do. That Jesus is the Son of God (divine) is evidenced throughout Scripture and history. But that He is the Son of man (human) is just as profoundly stated—seventy-seven times in the Bible.

Jesus Had Limitations

Jesus in His present state has great powers and immunities, but in His life upon earth, He had limitations like all humans. In John 4:6 we read that after walking several hours, Jesus' legs were tired, and He sat upon the edge of Jacob's well to rest. In Matt. 8:24, while sailing across the Sea of Galilee, He must have been very sleepy, for He slept during a storm that covered the boat with waves. In Matt. 21:18 Jesus must have had hunger pangs. And in John 19:28 He became very thirsty. Luke 22:44 records that while praying in the wooded park (Gethsemane) on the side of Mount Olivet, walking distance from the Temple in Jerusalem, He underwent extreme agony, to the point that "his sweat was as it were great drops of blood falling down to the ground."

And the Bible further tells us that Jesus underwent strong temptations of Satanic origin, temptations offering greatness and power (Matt. 4:1-12). But He resisted the temptations and chose the cross. How encouraging to know that Jesus was a human being with a face and human limitations just like our own, yet He turned His back upon temptations that He knew were not within God's desires.

Besides physical limitations, Jesus also had limitations

of power and limitations of an intellectual and moral nature. Yet all limitations, the natural laws, were self-imposed so that He might be totally and completely a man (Phil. 2:7-8).

The Bible also tells us that Jesus even got angry. (What! My Jesus showed anger?) The Bible calls it zeal, but it resulted in Jesus grabbing a rope and using it like a whip to chase the merchants and animals out of the Temple area, pouring out their money and overturning their tables. Mark 3:5 says Jesus "looked round about on them with anger." Anger is not sin but a characteristic of God, Jesus, and mankind to be used to fight sin and Satanic forces.

Laughter and Tears

When the seventy disciples whom Jesus had sent out to minister in His name returned with news of their successful ministry, Jesus "rejoiced in spirit" (Luke 10:21). I can see Him now, jumping and shouting and laughing with His followers. When you rejoice in the powerful Spirit of God, you can't do it standing still; joy spills out from within.

And when Jesus spoke, it was with gaiety and charm (Luke 4:22). What wit, humor, and irony adorned His speech when He told the Pharisees that they polish and clean the outside of their cups, but forget to clean the inside and strain the wine to keep out the gnats, but, taking a drink, gulp down a whole camel—long neck, hump, all four legs. There must have been a roar of laughter at that one.

Then Jesus hit them with another one from His repertoire, "Woe unto you, scribes and Pharisees, hypocrites! for ye are like unto whited sepulchres, which indeed appear beautiful outward, but are within full of dead men's bones, and of all uncleanness" (Matt. 23:27). Can't you see it: a Pharisee is like a shiny tomb polished to glitter in the streets of Jerusalem, but inside they are nothing but old dead bones and rats and things. If I had heard that one, I would have rolled in the streets with laughter. Did you ever think about the humorous side of Jesus? Indeed He was filled with all of man's traits and characteristics, including sorrow, as we see Him weeping over the city of Jerusalem from Mt. Olivet (Luke 19:41-44). Tears that say Jerusalem is doomed to destruction—the city that sings with a history of 2000 years of Hebrew heritage—now soon to be cut off.

It is recorded at least twenty-five times that Jesus prayed. This was His source of rejuvenation and guidance, as it is with man today. In Heb. 5:7-8 we read of Jesus' crying and the fear He possessed, and that He had to learn to be obedient just as we do. Jesus on earth did not possess an inherent omnipotence due to His divine nature but received His power through an anointing of the Holy Ghost from God (Acts 10:38), just like all men.

Features from the Bible

Jesus, being a man, had physical features. However, there is little specific information found in the Bible about His appearance. No doubt this was in God's plan, for it is man's nature to make paintings and statues of reverent figures objects of worship. God would not have us worshiping a statue or local look-alike.

Isaiah, prophesying 700 years before Jesus, says, "He hath no form nor comeliness; and when we shall see him, there is no beauty that we should desire him" (Isa. 53:2). Here Isaiah is describing the suffering of Jesus during

His trials, a time when He was beaten, spat upon, mocked, whipped, and rejected by the world He so dearly loved. Under those circumstances, He would naturally have no beauty.

In Gethsemane Judas had to greet Jesus with a kiss to identify Him to the crowd (Matt. 26:48). Does this suggest that His features were not outstanding, that He physically blended in with the crowd? The many accounts recorded of Jesus' actions certainly tell us of the remarkable eyes He must have possessed. Eyes that so often "looked upon" people, eyes that revealed the compassion and strength seen by those who were healed, eyes that supported the authority of His word, eyes that made men take Him seriously.

Some construe that because He was a carpenter and walked a couple of thousand miles on foot and carried a heavy cross on His shoulders and threw the crooked money changers out of the Temple, Jesus was a giant of a man. Jesus probably was a well-built, masculine, and strong man. He won the admiration of a large group of men, not to mention such women as Mary and Martha, who were very close to Him.

In Nazareth, Jesus boldly walked through a mob of hostile men who were about to throw Him from the brow of a hill. He remained untouched (Luke 4:28-30).

In Gethsemane, when Judas came with a band of men and officers to arrest Jesus, they asked for His whereabouts. Jesus boldly stated, "I am he," and when they looked, they all fell backwards to the ground (John 18:6). It is not likely they saw a small, frail man, but one of dignity, confidence, and perhaps great physical strength.

The words "power" and "authority" are often used in connection with Jesus. His followers had a great deal of respect for His courage, confidence, tireless traveling on foot over rugged hills, sleeping on cold grounds, and living the life of a rugged outdoorsman.

Single-handed, Jesus stood before organized groups such as the Pharisees and Sadducees and denounced them and their authority, eye to eye.

In Isa. 50:6 we read that Jesus had hair plucked from His face, indicating He may have worn a beard.

As for his having long hair, it is not likely. At least it wasn't as long as the Nazarites' hair, which hung long down their backs. Nazarites were members of a religious group that never cut their hair. Jesus was not a Nazarite, for He drank of the fruit of the vine (Mark 14:25), and touched the dead (Matt. 9:25). He was, however, a Nazarene, a person from the city of Nazareth. Jesus is considered not to have long hair, because He inspired Paul to write, "Doth not even nature itself teach you, that, if a man have long hair, it is a shame unto him" (1 Cor. 11:14).

Jesus' apparel most likely consisted of a tunic (a loose-fitting shirt that extended to the knees), a robe or mantle draped over the shoulders and bound about the waist by a girdle (wide belt), a turban for protection from the sun and cold, and a pair of sandals made of wood, leather, or felt. The Bible tells that a woman "touched the hem of his garment" (Matt. 9:20). The reference here is to a blue threaded lace or tassel that was commonly worn on the fringe of the robe to remind wearers of their heavenly Father (see Num. 15:37-40). Jesus probably wore such a blue fringe, and the afflicted reached to touch it for their healing (Matt. 14:36).

One exegete upon the life of Christ speculates that, based on Jesus' age and nationality, "we will not be very far out of the way when we picture Jesus as of medium height, olive complexion, closely cut hair, no beard, bright eyes, Jewish facial lines, gracious expression, of perfect health, of dignified appearance."

Features from Historical Writings

There are a few descriptions of Jesus' physical features found in historical writings supposedly dating from the first century. While there are overlapping features mentioned, there are also contradictory ones. These writings are generally considered spurious and are never to be considered inspired of God.

One such description comes to us from John of Damascus some 750 years after Jesus walked the flower-speckled hills of Galilee. Tradition says this description was handed down from the Apostle John through Polycarp, Papias, and Irenaeus. The Apostle John was the last of the twelve to die, living until the end of the first century. Perhaps there is some truth in the description that tells us Jesus had a beautiful face with an olive complexion resembling His mother. And that it expressed wisdom and nobility and that His hair was of curly locks.

Another description is a lengthy account from an unknown author, supposedly written during Jesus' lifetime:

There lives at this time in Judea a man of singular virtue, whose name is Jesus Christ, whom the barbarians esteem as a prophet, but his followers love and adore him as the offspring of the immortal God. He calls back the dead from the grave and heals all sorts of diseases with a word or touch. He is a tall man, well shaped, and of an amiable and reverend aspect; his hair of a color that can hardly be matched, falling in graceful curls, waving about and very agreeably couching upon his shoulders, parted on the crown of the head, running like a stream to the front after the fashion of the Nazarites; his forehead high, large and imposing; his cheeks without spot or wrinkle, beautiful with a lovely red; his nose and mouth formed with exquisite symmetry; his beard of the color of new wine suitable to his hair, reaching below his chin and parted in the middle like a fork; his eyes bright blue, clear, and serene, look innocent, dignified, manly, and mature. In proportion of body most perfect and captivating; his arms and hands delectable to behold. He rebukes with majesty, counsels with mildness; his whole address whether in word or deed, being eloquent and grave. No man has seen him laugh, yet his manners are exceedingly pleasant, but he has wept frequently in the presence of men. He is temperate, modest, and wise. A man for his extraordinary beauty and divine perfections, surpassing the children of men in every sense.

A letter from Lentulus, president of the people of Jerusalem, addressed to the first-century Roman Senate, says of Jesus:

A man of tall stature, beautiful, with venerable countenance, which they who look on it can both love and fear. His hair is waving, somewhat wine-colored; his brow is smooth and most serene; his face is without spot or wrinkle, and glows with a delicate flush; his nose and mouth are faultless, the beard is abundant and his eyes prominent and brilliant; in speech he is grave, reserved and modest.

This letter, however, is believed to have been written in the twelfth century.

The Archko Volume, Keats Publishing Inc., New Canaan, Connecticut, was originally published in 1887 as the "official documents made in these courts (Sanhedrin) in the days of Jesus Christ." The compiler, W.D. Mahan, states that he had these papers translated "from manuscripts in Constantinople and the records of the senatorial docket taken from the Vatican in Rome." He found these papers in the nineteenth century among thousands of books and writings in these two great and very old Christian libraries. The volume includes a report made by Gamaliel (see Acts 5:34), an honored and respected teacher of the Pharisees in the days of Christ, to the Sanhedrin at Jerusalem. In this report we read, concerning Jesus:

He is the picture of his mother, only he has not her smooth, round face. His hair is a little more golden than hers, though it is as much from sunburn as anything else. He is tall, and his shoulders are a little drooped; his visage is thin and of a swarthy complexion, though this is from exposure. His eyes are large and a soft blue, and rather dull and heavy. The lashes are long, and his eyebrows very large. His nose is that of a Jew. In fact he reminds me of an old-fashioned Jew in every sense of the word.

Also from the *Archko Volume* we find a report made to Caesar by Pontius Pilate concerning the events of the crucifixion, entitled "Acta Pilati," or the Acts of Pilate. In this we read:

His golden-colored hair and beard gave to his appearance a celestial aspect. He appeared to be about thirty years of age. Never have I seen a sweeter or more serene countenance. What a contrast between him and his hearers, with their black beards and tawny complexions.

Features from Artwork

As far as actual paintings of Jesus are concerned, there have been thousands made down through the years. Most all are products of the artist's imagination. The earlier ones, those of the first 300 years, in nearly every case picture Jesus without a beard. These paintings, many of which are frescos painted on the walls and ceilings of the catacombs, often depict various stories in the life of Jesus.

The catacombs are underground tunnels where the dead were buried to avoid cremation during the first couple of centuries A.D. Some are over five stories deep and have over ten miles of passageways. Christians under Roman persecution hid like ants in these subterranean passageways. Any artwork found on the walls is likely to depict some strong element of their faith, possibly even the image of the Lord for whom they were giving their lives.

One such fresco was found on the ceiling of a vault in the catacombs of Rome. In 1847 a British portraitist, Thomas Heaphy, copied the faded fresco with the utmost reverential care. The copy was found in 1932 in the British Museum by Rev. C.C. Dobson. The vault is known to date to the first century.

Also found in the Roman catacombs is a mosaic profile of the head of Christ expressing similar features.

Another early painting of Christ, dating to the second century, is found on a cloth in the Church of S. Bartolomeo in Genoa, Italy.

Still another, the head of Christ painted on cypress wood, is traditionally attributed to Luke. It is now at the Vatican in Rome and is considered to be of third-century origin.

The similarity of these paintings is obvious. They each depict Jesus with a high, smooth forehead; long, dark hair with slightly parted beard and moustache; long, slender nose; large, passionate eyes with long slanting eyebrows; high cheekbones, small mouth, and narrow chin. The similarities indicate that each had access to a prototype, or that one was copied from another, or that each was painted from the verbal description of Jesus passed along with the gospel.

The Image on the Shroud

Perhaps the most astonishing portrait of Jesus that exists today is the image that appears on a fourteen-foot by three-foot linen cloth sealed in a vault at the Cathedral of Turin in Italy. This cloth is believed to be the shroud draped over Jesus at His burial and found by Peter and John at the tomb after the Resurrection (John 20:3-7). The shroud is believed to have been preserved by the apostles and the early church.

The recorded history of the shroud began in France in 1353. It was placed in its present location in Turin, Italy, in 1532. In 1898 it was removed and photographed for the first time. The chemical process of the then-new science of photography was able to pick up stains in the cloth previously unseen by the naked eye. As the first photograph lay in the developing tray, an astounding image slowly came forth. The photo showed stains that marked the entire front and back image of a man who had been whipped, crowned with thorns, crucified, speared in the side, and who had supported on his back and shoulder a tremendous weight. The image on the cloth is a negative itself, so that a photographic negative reveals it as a positive. This would be the exact case of a cloth stained from the underside in such a manner.

Exactly what made the stains no one knows for sure, perhaps body oils; or as some have postulated, the physical change of Jesus' body to immortality at the resurrection could have released a brief yet violent burst of some type of radiation, which could have scorched or stained the cloth.

In 1931 the cloth was again removed and numerous official photographs were taken. These are held by The Holy Shroud Guild in New York and have been the basis of much study.

Air Force Academy science instructors, pathologists at leading medical universities, and numerous other scientists have recently studied the shroud. It has been shown that the man whose image appears on the linen was crucified with nails through each of his wrists and one through his overlapping feet. Had the nails gone through his hands they would have pulled out. The man most likely died of asphyxiation due to the position of the suspended body on the cross. It has been shown that the man was about five feet ten inches tall and weighed perhaps 175 pounds.

But the real sensation comes when we compare the image of the face on the shroud with the ones that were painted in the first and second century. All of the common features are there—the high forehead, the long nose.

Even more exciting is the possibility that the painters painted the verbally given picture of Jesus and 1900 years later these portraits are validated by the Holy Shroud, the only real and authentic photo ever taken of Jesus, and taken by Jesus himself. Could this be a twentieth-century gift from God?

7

The final day of reckoning came when Jesus died on the cross and his dead body was sealed in a tomb. Could He defeat death as He had promised? It looked doubtful; still they waited. All of Christianity hung upon what happened next.

Did Jesus Rise from the Dead?

It was John Wesley's father who said, "The inward witness, son, the inward witness, this is the proof, the strongest proof of Christianity." But to the millions of logic-minded people throughout the world who want very much to believe that Christ actually rose from the dead, but have never felt an inward witness, God has left a solid chain of logical evidence that His Son did resurrect.

Jesus, during His life on earth, claimed many times to be the Son of God (John 4:25-26; 10:7-11; 16:27-28). These claims are backed by great miracles, hundreds of fulfilled prophecies, and eye-opening *types* (events symbolic of Christ) from the Old Testament. But God gave the ultimate proof by raising his Son from the dead. In Rom. 1:4 we read that Jesus was by His resurrection "declared to be the Son of God. . . ." The declaration was made by God.

A series of interlocking links collectively binds the evidence that Jesus physically rose from the dead. This irrefutable evidence from history can loosen our intellectual defenses against the resurrection. Then God can enter and unite with our spirits, and from within bear witness to our intellect that this event is indeed true.

He Was Dead

To begin, we must ascertain the fact that Jesus actually *died* on the cross. Some would have us believe He only fainted and later revived. However, the Roman government *certified* His death.

> And Pilate marvelled if he were already dead: and calling unto him the centurion, he asked him whether he had been any while dead. And when he knew it of the centurion, he gave the body to Joseph. (Mark 15:44-45)

After what Pilate had been through, there is no chance he would have released the body not knowing *for sure* Jesus was dead.

The centurion was not the only one who witnessed this death. Dr. Luke names many: the people, his acquaintances, women of Galilee. Jesus' dead body was not left unattended. There is not a shred of evidence that any of these Roman, Greek, or Jewish witnesses ever suspected he had merely fainted.

> And all the people that came together to that sight, beholding the things which were done, smote their breasts, and returned. And all his acquaintance, and the women that followed him from Galilee, stood afar off, beholding these things. (Luke 23:48-49)

Often before crucified people were removed from the cross, their legs were broken to speed up the death. But with Jesus, the Roman soldiers saw and *knew* He was dead. One soldier bled Jesus' body by laying the point of his sharp spear along his rib cage and thrusting it into

His heart to bring forth a gush of blood. This effect would have been similar to cutting the jugular vein of slaughtered cattle. The Apostle John was standing close and saw the entire event.

Then came the soldiers, and broke the legs of the first, and of the other which was crucified with him. But when they came to Jesus, and saw that he was dead already, they brake not his legs: But one of the soldiers with a spear pierced his side, and forthwith came there out blood and water. And he that saw it bare record, and his record is true: and he knoweth that he saith true, that ye might believe. (John 19:32-35)

At three o'clock in the afternoon Jesus died. Shortly thereafter, two *well-respected* Pharisees—Joseph of Arimathea, a rich man (Matt. 27:57) and "an honourable counsellor" (Mark 15:43), and Nicodemus, a well-respected (John 7:50-51) ruler of the Jews (John 3:1)—actually lifted and hand-carried the limp body of Jesus to the tomb, where the body was cleaned and wrapped with yards of linen cloth (John 19:39-40). Surely they would have detected some sign of life if there was any. Because of Jerusalem's altitude and warm season, and due to the great loss of blood on the cross, the body of Jesus would already have become stiff from rigor mortis before the men left Him at six o'clock in the evening. A body still warm and limp after three hours surely would have brought suspicion to those at the tomb.

The disciples' written record, supported by the expectations for human nature, makes it most evident that Jesus was in fact *dead* before being placed in the tomb.

Tomb Officially Sealed

The second major evidence for Jesus' resurrection is

that the tomb in which Jesus was placed was *sealed*. In the manner of the times, after the body was placed inside, a great stone was rolled over the opening of the hewn-out tomb (Matt. 27:60). Then the chief priests and Pharisees, fearing the disciples would steal Jesus' body and claim He resurrected, requested the Roman government make the tomb sure by stretching a cord across its entrance and placing a wad of clay showing the Roman seal at the ends of the cord. This was the manner in which Rome made it illegal for anyone to enter the tomb. And to further guard against a plot of deception, guards were placed to watch over the tomb. While the guards and the seal were not placed until the next morning, the tomb would have been inspected for occupancy before placing the seal.

Now the next day, that followed the day of the preparation, the chief priests and Pharisees came together unto Pilate, Saying, Sir, we remember that that deceiver said, while he was yet alive, After three days I will rise again. Command therefore that the sepulchre be made sure until the third day, lest his disciples come by night, and steal him away, and say unto the people, He is risen from the dead: so the last error shall be worse than the first. Pilate said unto them, Ye have a watch: go your way, make it as sure as ye can. So they went, and made the sepulchre sure, sealing the stone, and setting a watch. (Matt. 27:62-66)

There is no question that Jesus was dead and His body was inside the sealed tomb.

Tomb Positively Identified
Some claim that on the morning of the third day Mary

returned to a *different* tomb and found it empty. But evidence reveals that she returned to the very same tomb in which Jesus had been placed. The tomb was in a *conspicuous* location in a garden very close to the mount of the crucifixion (John 19:41-42). Several women, including Mary Magdalene and Jesus' mother, witnessed placing the body in the tomb and were familiar with its location (Luke 23:55; Mark 15:47). The tomb was owned by the man who wrapped and placed Jesus' body, Joseph of Arimathea (Matt. 27:59-61). Surely he would have returned to witness the empty tomb and to ascertain its location. Perhaps even hundreds who had witnessed the crucifixion and burial would have returned to see the empty tomb, for this event was of no minor significance.

Angels Were Seen

Then a most peculiar thing occurred. At dawn on Sunday morning after the Sabbath (Saturday),

> There was a great earthquake: for the angel of the Lord descended from heaven, and came and rolled back the stone from the door, and sat upon it. His countenance was like lightning, and his raiment white as snow: And for fear of him the keepers did shake, and become as dead men. And the angel answered and said unto the women, Fear not ye: for I know that ye seek Jesus, which was crucified. He is not here: for he is risen, as he said. Come, see the place where the Lord lay. (Matt. 28:2-6)

The first seed of the Christian faith had germinated— had come out of the ground. The news came early Sunday morning on April 7, A.D. 30. "He is risen "; the words of Mary Magdalene filled the room. Peter and John

71

dashed out the door to inspect the tomb. The others stood in silent awe—"and oh, the joy that floods my soul!"

Notice several things here. The angel and the rolling of the stone was witnessed by the guards as well as by the two Marys who had come to the tomb. Not only does the Bible say so, but the detailed description of the event as given to the writer Matthew is that of an eye witness. The angel spoke to them all, calling Jesus "the Lord" and witnessing to the fact that "he is risen."

The angel did not free Jesus; *He was already gone.* The angel came to remove the stone and to bear witness as to why the body was no longer there. The first witness of the now risen Lord Jesus was an angel, who explained it all and showed the proof.

Hundreds Saw Jesus After Resurrection

As if the witness of an angel was not enough, Jesus remained on the earth forty days after the resurrection. He did not immediately ascend into heaven but walked the land and talked to many people. The Apostle John says Jesus performed many signs to these people to prove He was the resurrected Jesus.

And many other signs truly did Jesus in the presence of his disciples, which are not written in this book: But these are written, that ye might believe that Jesus is the Christ, the Son of God; and that believing ye might have life through his name. (John 20:30-31)

Dr. Luke in writing the book of Acts emphatically states:

He shewed himself alive after his passion by many

infallible proofs, being seen of them forty days, and speaking of the things pertaining to the kingdom of God. (Acts 1:3)

The body in which Jesus appeared could eat (Luke 24:42-43), could be touched (Luke 24:38-40), and could pass through closed doors (John 20:19).

The Bible records that Jesus made at least twelve appearances after His resurrection: to Mary Magdalene (Mark 16:9; John 20:15-16); several women at the tomb (Matt. 28:9); two disciples on the road to Emmaus, a town about eight miles west of Jerusalem (Luke 24:13-32); Peter (Luke 24:34; 1 Cor. 15:5); ten disciples (John 20:19); eleven disciples (John 20:26); and after the second Sunday to seven on the shore of the Sea of Galilee, some ninety miles north of the resurrection site in Jerusalem (John 21:1-22); eleven disciples on a hilltop in Galilee (Matt. 28:16); twelve disciples, including Matthias (Acts 1:26; 1 Cor. 15:5); at least one appearance to 500 followers at once (1 Cor. 15:6); then to His brother James (1 Cor. 15:7; Gal. 1:19).

Ascension Witnessed

Then, at the end of the forty-day ministry, Jesus led His followers to the Mount of Olives, just east of Jerusalem. There, while they watched, His feet lifted off the ground, and they witnessed His ascension up into the clouds (Acts 1:9-11).

Not once throughout the rest of their lives did any of these people ever doubt having seen Jesus in the flesh after the resurrection. Many of them died a painful death of martyrdom while profoundly witnessing to the very end that Jesus had risen from the dead and thereby proved himself the Son of God.

1 Cor. 15:32 raises an important question. If Christ did not rise from the dead, then neither will we, so we have nothing to gain from Christianity. We might as well eat and drink in the evils of the world, for tomorrow we die and it's all over. *But* verse 33 says, "Be not deceived." There is far more for us than just life on earth. God proved this for us by resurrecting Jesus and surrounding this event with infallible evidence, so that even the nonbeliever can believe and thus become a child of God.

Old Testament Hints

In 1 Cor. 15:4, Paul said of Jesus, "that he rose again the third day according to the scriptures." Paul was referring to the Old Testament, "the scriptures" of Paul's day. Paul is saying the Old Testament told him Jesus would resurrect on the third day. Paul was referring to typology, because Jesus was not yet born when the Old Testament was written. There are a number of symbolic types God revealed in the Old Testament that foretell actual events in the New Testament (see 1 Cor. 10:6). God put these types in the Bible so we would know the Bible is not a product of man but of God himself.

Noah's Ark Hints of the Resurrection

Noah's ark is a type that represents the tomb, with the Spirit of God inside (the eight believers) and the waves of death beating against the outside. As the ark finally came to rest on Mt. Ararat, Noah came forth into the light of a new world. See how God has shown us that, in a like manner, His Son in the tomb would pass through the turbulent waters of death and emerge safely to walk into the light? Noah's actions prefigure the resurrection.

And as if that were not enough, God inspired the recorder to add the exact day the ark came to rest on Mt. Ararat. It was the seventeenth day of the seventh month (see Gen. 8:4). In Noah's day, the seventh month was *Abib (Nisan)*, which was later changed to become the first month (Exod. 12:2). We know that it was the fourteenth day of this month (Nisan) that the sacrificial lamb was slain (Lev. 23:5). God's sacrificial lamb, Jesus, was also slain this same date (mere coincidence?). And three days later, He resurrected; three days later becomes the seventeenth day of the seventh month (mere coincidence?). Three thousand years after Noah passed through the waters of death and emerged from the ark to walk into the light, bringing with him the first generations (the animals and his children) of the new world, *on exactly the same day*, Jesus passed through death, emerged from the tomb, walked into the morning light, and became the first one resurrected of a new generation of people—Christians—in a new world (mere coincidence?).

Feast of Firstfruits, Another Sign

In the Feast of Firstfruits ordered by God in Lev. 23:10, Moses directs the Israelite priests to take a sheaf of the first harvest and wave it before the people on the day after the Sabbath. The wheat emerged from a seed planted in the earth. In this manner the people would be reminded that God is able to bring forth life from the earth. The day chosen (by God) was the day after the Saturday (Sabbath) after Passover—the exact same day (1500 years later) that Jesus resurrected. Isn't it obvious that God was pretelling the story of His Son? Jesus would be planted in the earth as a seed, and on the day after the

Sabbath after Passover, He would be plucked out of the earth and shown to the people as proof that God is able to resurrect life. The New Testament verifies this in stating, "Now is Christ risen from the dead, and become the firstfruits of them that slept" (1 Cor. 15:20). You and I are the remaining seed, and Jesus' resurrection is a guarantee of our resurrection. The thousands of seeds we see germinated every day—weeds, vegetable, flowers, and trees—remind us that God is able to bring life out of the ground.

Aaron's Rod is the Resurrected Jesus

The budding of Aaron's rod is yet another foreshadowing of Jesus' resurrection. In Numbers 17, God speaks to Moses and tells him to bring forth twelve rods, one from each of the twelve tribes, and place them in the Tabernacle. The rod from the tribe of Levi was to have Aaron's name on it. In the morning Moses came (just as the women came and found Jesus alive) and found the rod was "alive." It had budded, flowered, and produced fruit. The live rod was then shown to the people (just as Jesus was) to prove Aaron was God's chosen one (just as Jesus was). The resurrection of the rod was God's proof of Aaron, and the resurrection of Jesus is God's proof that Jesus is Lord. In the book of Acts the great message that went out from Jerusalem to all the lands was centered around the resurrection as *proof* of Jesus' deity.

Ceremonial Hint

The cleansing of the leper is another type of Jesus' resurrection. In Leviticus 14 we read that if a leper's symptoms disappear, he can be pronounced clean by the priest, who makes the following ceremony: Take two live birds. Kill one and spill his blood in an earthen vessel. Dip the remaining live bird in the blood, sprinkle it on the leper seven times, then set the bird free to fly to the heavens. Here we see a foreshadowing of the crucifixion of Jesus, the spilling of his blood, the burial in an earthen vessel (tomb), and the second bird as representing the resurrection of Jesus as He ascends to heaven, stained with blood, yet free.

Passing Through the Jordan

When the children of Israel ceased their forty-year wandering and proceeded to enter the promised land (Israel) under the leadership of Joshua, they entered from the east and crossed through the Jordan River. As they stepped into the waters, the river stopped flowing, and all the Israelites entered, passed through untouched by the waters, and came out the other side clean and dry (Josh. 3).

This whole event again showed Christ entering into the tomb untouched by death's sting and emerging victoriously in the resurrection. To amplify this God had the children of Israel construct a stone monument in the middle of the river as a symbol of death to the old world, then to construct a second monument on the new shore as a symbol of emerging free into the light of the new land. This is still another guarantee that we too will someday pass through death and emerge into a new world just as Jesus did, just as Joshua did, just as the children of Israel did. But for now we must continue to wander in the wilderness. Jordan is ahead of us.

Hints of the Three Days

The Bible has many events centered around the

number three, to tell us that Jesus would be in the grave three days. Jonah was in the belly of the fish for three days. And this is stated by Jesus in Matt. 12:40 as a sign that He would be in the belly of the earth for three days.

The request of the children of Israel to depart Egypt and go "three days journey into the desert" to sacrifice to the Lord is a symbol of God's other child, Jesus, who departed for three days from this world (Exod. 5:3).

In Num. 10:33 we see the ark of the covenent going before the wandering children of Israel in a three days' journey to seek a resting place. While Jesus was three days departed from the earth, the Bible says He (His soul) also journeyed into the lower parts of the earth (Eph. 4:9) before emerging from the tomb to a resting place. The ark was a large, ornate chest that carried the tablet of the Ten Commandments, a cup of manna, and Aaron's rod that budded (Heb. 9:4). God has shown that this 1500 B.C. event of Aaron's resurrected rod, in the ark, on a three-day journey, leading the children of Israel to a resting place, is in fact an allusion to the story of Jesus in the tomb on a three-day journey to lead Christians to a place of rest.

Isaac, the Resurrected Jesus

Perhaps the greatest event of the Old Testament that tells the story of Jesus' resurrection is found in Gen. 22:1-18. Here Abraham, in obedience to God, takes his only son, Isaac, on a three-day journey to the hills of Jerusalem to offer him as a sacrifice upon an altar. But Isaac was permitted to live. To Abraham, his son was dead for three days (from the time he was told he must kill him to the time he was told not to kill him). What an accurate foretelling of the story of God, who spared not

78

His only Son, who was sacrificed and was dead to the world for three days, but who was also returned (as was Isaac). Heb. 11:19 speaks of this event as a figure or type of the resurrection.

Joash, Another Hint

One additional event that occurred around 800 B.C. clearly depicts the salvation of Jesus and our relationship to him today (see 2 Kings 11). Jezebel's daughter, Athaliah, killed all of the royal seed and took the throne of Judah. Unknown to her, one "from among the slain" was hidden to await the day he would be rightly placed on the throne. This spared child, Joash, was the only one left in the bloodline of the promised Messiah. The Levites (the church) were the only ones who knew he was alive, and they waited in anticipated joy for the day he would be given the throne. Here again we have the story of Jesus, who was spared. But it is only the Christians (the church) who know this, and we wait with great enthusiasm for the day of His return, when He will take the throne of His kingdom, just as Joash did in his symbolic event.

Conclusion

The resurrection of Jesus is not a fairy tale or a product of man's desirous imagination, but a profound truth of life foretold, foreshadowed, and carried through by God just as He planned from the beginning. The day the Son came up has to be the greatest day on earth—the crowning evidence that all God has told us is true and that the Bible is in fact the Holy Bible.

8

In today's "enlightened" society it is very easy to pass off the virgin birth as just another fable that has no real significance to Christianity. If you were told you might not have salvation if you did not accept the virgin birth, would you take a closer look?

Was Jesus Really Born of a Virgin?

Often we hear in Christian circles discussion of the virgin birth as fact or fable. To accept this event as fable is a dangerous thought. If Jesus was not born of a virgin the cornerstone of the Christian faith would dissolve, and the entire superstructure of Christianity would crumble.

By studying the Bible we can observe three facts about God's system within which we live. And from these three facts we must conclude that Jesus *had to be born of a virgin.* Even if the Bible did not tell us He was (and it does), the virgin birth was an absolute necessity. Here are the three facts.

Fact #1: Sin and death entered the world
When Adam was created as the first spiritual man on earth, he was made to have eternal fellowship with God. However, this automatic salvation granted to Adam and his descendants was contingent upon obedience. Disobedience would cause a separation from God. The Bible calls it death, and indeed it is.

> But of the fruit of the tree which is in the midst of the garden, God hath said, Ye shall not eat of it, neither shall ye touch it, lest ye die. (Gen. 3:3)

The fruit wasn't poison to touch or eat; by "die" God was referring to eternal damnation, death of the spirit caused by separation.

And needless to say, true to the nature of man, Adam disobeyed.

> And the man said, The woman whom thou gavest to be with me, she gave me of the tree, and I did eat. (Gen. 3:12)

Adam's disobedience marked the "fall of man." Because the first man sinned—Adam, the father of us all—sin entered the world. And with sin came death.

> For the wages of sin is death. (Rom. 6:23)

The death was not just for Adam. As the father of our race, it was passed on to us all.

> Wherefore, as by one man sin entered into the world, and death by sin; and so death passed upon all men, for that all have sinned. (Rom. 5:12)

At that point all of mankind was headed for an eternity in the grave. However, God loved man too much to just leave him to perish, so He established a bypass: the *sacrificial system*, through which man could eliminate his sin by transferring it into the body of an unblemished lamb sacrificed upon an altar.

Fact #2: Blood sacrifice puts away sin and death

God introduced the blood sacrifice to Adam in the garden. Adam had tried to cover his nakedness with fig leaves.

> And the eyes of them both were opened, and they

knew that they were naked; and they sewed fig leaves together, and made themselves aprons. (Gen. 3:7)

But God *spilled the blood* of animals and made clothes of their skin to hide Adam's nakedness.

Unto Adam also and to his wife did the Lord God make coats of skins, and clothed them. (Gen. 3:21)

Even as early as this God introduced to man the necessity of the spilled blood to hide or put away sin.

Thus began the sacrificial system, ordained by God not man, whereby sin could be put away and provision made for salvation. Recall that shortly afterwards Cain's fruit sacrifice was not accepted by God but Abel's animal was.

Cain brought of the fruit of the ground an offering unto the Lord. And Abel, he also brought of the firstlings of his flock and of the fat thereof. And the Lord had respect unto Abel and to his offering: But unto Cain and to his offering he had not respect. (Gen. 4:3-5)

A few thousand years later, God gave specific instructions to His people in bondage in Egypt concerning their freedom. He said they were to sacrifice an *unblemished* lamb.

Your lamb shall be without blemish. (Exod. 12:5)

Then he said to smear the blood of the lamb outside the door to show obedience.

And they shall take of the blood, and strike it on the two side posts and on the upper door post of the houses, wherein they shall eat it. (Exod. 12:7)

83

The death angel, upon seeing this sign of obedience, the applied blood, would not enter.

> And the blood shall be to you for a token upon the houses where ye are: and when I see the blood, I will pass over you, and the plague shall not be upon you to destroy you, when I smite the land of Egypt. (Exod. 12:13)

In other words, obedience to God in accepting the blood of the lamb would literally defeat death and set them free from bondage in Egypt.

God had introduced this system of the sacrificial blood to prepare His people, and the world, for the one great sacrifice that would put away Adam's sin forever; but He needed an umblemished human sacrifice to put away human sin.

Fact #3: None of Adam's descendants would do

In the Rom. 5:12 passage we saw that all of Adam's descendants are born with his sin in their blood: "by one man . . . death passed upon all men." For God's ultimate sacrifice, the one He had been preparing the Hebrew people for, He needed an "unblemished lamb," a human who had no sin in his blood. No mere man has ever been righteous enough to fill this role.

> As it is written, There is none righteous, no, not one. (Rom. 3:10)

> For all have sinned, and come short of the glory of God. (Rom. 3:23)

Even babies, who appear so innocent, are born with this poison in their blood:

How then can man be justified with God? or how can he be clean that is born of a woman? (Job 25:4)

There was only one solution. There must be a human being born into the world who was *not* begotten by a descendant of Adam. God himself must beget a son who is free from all ancient sin and who would live a sinless, unblemished life.

The Necessity of the Virgin Birth

Now we are beginning to see why the virgin birth became a necessity. Only through a Holy Spirit conception could Jesus bypass the sin that was passing through all the inhabitants of the earth.

If Jesus did not go upon the cross a sinless, unblemished lamb, then He could not have atoned for the sin of the world. And if Adam's sin is not put away, neither is death. Jesus *proved* His purity and His *virgin birth* by coming out of the grave, leaving Adam's sin buried. Jesus could not have defeated death if He had any sin in His background.

Can we defeat death, too? We sure can, simply by being obedient to God and applying the blood of the lamb over our door. Thus we show the world we accept His unblemished, virgin-born lamb, whose blood was spilled on the cross to atone for *our* sin. Simply call upon His name (Rom. 10:10) and believe that He was unblemished (was virgin-born and lived a sinless life).

This brings us to the perfect time to quote the most famous phrase in the Bible, what has been called the "Bible in a verse," a passage penned by a man who became the first disciple of Jesus, who leaned on Him at the Last Supper, who stood at the foot of the cross, who was the first to enter the empty tomb, who cared for Mary after Jesus ascended, who was the last apostle to die, and who wrote five books of the New Testament—the beloved John.

For God so loved the world, that he gave his only begotten Son, that whosoever believeth in him should not perish, but have everlasting life. (John 3:16)

We can now conclude that belief in the virgin birth, to produce an "unblemished lamb" who has the capacity to atone sin, is the only road to salvation. Naturally we must all go to the grave, but only our body goes if we have received the lamb, and then for just a short time.

Additional Proof
Before departing this subject, let's look at a few paraphrased Scripture verses that illuminate and complement the conclusion we have reached.

God did not send Jesus to condemn the world but to save it (John 3:17). The reason Jesus came was to put away sin, the work of the devil (1 John 3:8). Jesus is able to grant salvation to those who come to God through Him. Jesus became one of us but is *separate from sinners* (Heb. 7:25-26). This separation is due to the Holy Spirit conception—the virgin birth. It is the blood of Jesus (spilled on the cross as the ultimate sacrifice) that cleanses us from *all* sin (1 John 1:7-10).

The Bible tells of a virgin birth prophetically and historically, documented in the sacred annals of the Jewish people.

A virgin will bear a son and this will be God's sign (Isa. 7:14). An angel of the Lord tells Joseph in a dream that that which is in Mary is *conceived by the Holy Spirit*

(Matt. 1:20). Joseph had no intercourse with Mary until after Jesus was born (Matt. 1:25). The *virgin's* name was Mary (Luke 1:27). Mary admits to being a virgin (Luke 1:34). It was the power of the Highest which *overshadowed Mary* to produce a holy thing who was to be called the *Son of God* (Luke 1:35). Jesus, the Word who existed with God in the beginning, became flesh with us and was beheld as the Son of God (John 1:1, 14). God gave His *only begotten son* (John 3:16). God begat Jesus, not Joseph. Also recall Luke 1:37, "For with God nothing shall be impossible."

Further recall the Apostle's Creed, once believed to have been composed by the early apostles, "conceived by the Holy Ghost, born of the virgin Mary." The virgin birth was an integral part of the belief of the founding Church Fathers.

The *Acts of Pilate*, an A.D. 300 apocryphal book, tells of twelve who testified that Jesus was *not* born out of fornication and that Joseph and Mary were married. These men were obviously lying in order to have their rabbi freed. But the significance here is that the virgin birth was considered at Jesus' trials and is not a modern-day fable.

Believe on Jesus today and the Bible promises that you will be set free from bondage in the world (fear, anxiety, depression). You will be given abundant life on earth (John 10:10) and everlasting life when you pass through death (John 3:16).

9

Tradition, commercialism, and local adaptation give us many assorted (and sometimes distorted) stories of Jesus' birth. You may be surprised when you read . . .

The Truth About the Christmas Story

A Jesuit priest living among the Huron Indians in early America taught: "Within a lodge of broken bark the tender babe was found. A rugged robe of rabbit skin enwrapped his beauty round. The chiefs from far before him knelt with gifts of fox and beaver pelt. Jesus your king is born. Jesus is born in excelsis gloria."

Our own children learn many modern folk songs that relay the Christmas message. But we must remember that it is the character of folk tales, ballads, and legends to distort and amplify in order to seek the gut level or essence of a particular story or person.

While such presentations are enlightening and illuminate a certain characteristic of their subject not evident otherwise, we must be very careful not to apply it too seriously to Bible stories. The Bible is our only source of written truth; all else is speculation based upon observations. If we distort our Bible stories, we bend our only arrow of truth.

The Bible gives us the true account of the Christmas story, yet today we rarely read to see what it really says. How well do you know the Christmas story?

Following is a quiz about the Christmas story. Sharpen your pencil and mark each statement true or false. Then read the answers and comments.

1. Jesus had visitors who came from the Orient. T. F.
2. These visitors were kings. T. F.
3. There were three of them. T. F.
4. They came to visit Jesus lying in the manger. T. F.
5. A star led them to Bethlehem. T. F.
6. Their names were Casper, Melchoir, T. F.
   and Balthaser.
7. These men represented the white race, the T. F.
   yellow race, and the black race.
8. Joseph's home town was Nazareth. T. F.
9. After Jesus' birth, the first family move T. F.
   was to flee to Egypt.
10. Jesus' mother, Mary, was of pure T. F.
    Hebrew bloodline.
11. Swaddling clothes are rags used to wipe T. F.
    down animal sweat.
12. John the Baptist was born just six months T. F.
    ahead of Jesus, also in the town of Bethlehem.
13. Jesus had at least four brothers and T. F.
    two sisters.
14. Jesus' native tongue was Hebrew, the common T. F.
    language of the day.
15. Jesus' mother, Mary, and John the Baptist's T. F.
    mother, Elizabeth, were cousins, making Jesus
    and John the Baptist third cousins.
16. Jesus and John the Baptist knew each T. F.
    other well.
17. At birth, Mary bound Jesus in strips of cloth T. F.
    like a mummy to straighten His body
    for forty days.
18. The land into which Jesus was born T. F.
    was called Palestine.
19. Jesus' name was Jesus. T. F.

20. Jesus spoke Greek and Latin.   T. F.
21. Joseph died before Jesus began His ministry.   T. F.
22. Mary bought Jesus from God for $3.25.   T. F.
23. Mary rode nearly 100 miles on a donkey's   T. F.
    back just before she gave birth to Jesus.
24. Jesus was born December 25 in the year   T. F.
    zero, based on today's calendar.
25. The Christmas story is recorded in   T. F.
    all four Gospels.

Now let's see how well you did.

1. *False.* Jesus did have visitors, but they were not from the Orient. Matt. 2:1 says they came to Jerusalem from the east. The reference is to the east of Judea. It is generally believed they came from Mesopotamia, about 1000 miles east of Judea, in what is now western Iran. The "Orient" idea comes to us from the popular nineteenth-century folk song that reads, "We three kings of Orient are bearing gifts . . ."

2. *False.* This same folk song is also responsible for the idea that they were kings. Matthew is the only Gospel writer who tells the story of these visitors, and he calls them *magoi* or magi. It is usually interpreted *wise men.* These wise men were priestly advisors to kings. They based their knowledge upon star gazing, dream interpretation, divination, and other mystical phenomena. A modern-day counterpart is an astrologer, palm reader, magician (magi), or sorcerer. Such practice was commonly employed throughout Bible days (as it unfortunately is employed today). We find them in common practice in the days of Joseph in Egypt in 1720 B.C. (Gen. 41:8), when Moses stood before Pharaoh in 1500 B.C. (Exod. 7:11), and

in the days of Israel's first king, Saul, in 1000 B.C. (1 Sam. 28:7). They were used by King Nebuchadnezzar in 600 B.C. (Dan. 2:2), and are found in the first century A.D. (Acts 8:9). The Bible condemns all such practice (1 Sam. 15:23; Acts 19:19). But in this one special case, these wise men were chosen by God. They were of a learned class important enough to be summoned by Herod. Their arrival in Judea was a major event and caused much concern. God used the talents and position of these men to announce that His Son was in the world.

3. *False.* The Bible never says there were three, but that three *gifts* were brought. There could have been a dozen, for all we know. Considering their wealth, the great distance they traveled, and the number of robbers en route, it is likely there were many in the entourage, perhaps hundreds.

4. *False.* They did not come to the stable where Jesus was born. The Bible says they visited Him in a house, not when He was an infant but when He was a *young child.* Many speculate that since the wise men would have taken many weeks to travel to Judea, and because Herod ordered the death of all those *two years old and younger* (Matt. 2:16), and because the stable was only a temporary abode, Jesus was actually living in Nazareth with His folks and was perhaps one or two years old at the time of the wise men's visit. Perhaps your ceramic wise men are out of place in the manger scene under your Christmas tree.

5. Also *false.* The Bible says the star led them to Jerusalem (Matt. 2:1-2). Herod sent them to Bethlehem, but we are not told that is where they went. The Bible says the star "went before them, till it came and stood over where the young child was" (Matt. 2:9).

6. *False.* The names Casper, Melchoir, and Balthaser come from Hollywood imagination. The Bible reveals no names for the wise men.

7. *False.* We are given no indication of their national origin, but it is likely they were all from the same country.

8. *False.* Joseph was from Bethlehem. He had to go to his home town to register for taxation.

9. *False.* The first family move was to travel north to Jerusalem. When Jesus was eight days old, He was circumcised in the synagogue in Bethlehem. On the forty-first day the holy family traveled north to Jerusalem for Mary's purification (Lev. 12:1-6) and to present Jesus in the Temple (Luke 2:22). Since Mary gave a pair of turtle doves (a sign of the poorer class) instead of a lamb, we can assume the wise men had not yet visited them and given the rich gifts. Luke 2:39 says after they finished these rites, they returned to Galilee (the region in which Nazareth was located), not Bethlehem. The wise men must have visited them at home in Nazareth. One of the reasons for this visitation was to supply the holy family with the gold necessary for their flight and stay in Egypt.

10. *False.* Mary, like Joseph, was of the lineage of King David. David's great-grandmother was Ruth, a Moabitess who married the Jew Boaz. Neither David nor Mary nor Jesus was born of pure Hebrew stock. Perhaps this is just one subtle way in which God says it is not where you come from that counts, but where you are going.

11. *False.* Swaddling clothes are bands of narrow strips of cloth. Look this one up in your dictionary.

12. *False.* While John was born six months ahead of Jesus (Luke 1:26), the Bible does not name his home town, only that it was a city in the hill country of Judea

(Luke 1:39). Tradition says he was born in Ein Karem, a village near Jerusalem, while some say Hebron, seventeen miles south of Jerusalem.

13. *True.* Matt. 13:55-56 names His four half-brothers: James, Joses, Simon, and Judas, and says He had sisters (more than one). Jesus, however, was the firstborn of Mary.

14. *False.* Jesus' native tongue was Aramaic, a dialect of Hebrew. Hebrew was only used in the synagogue by the priest in Jesus' day.

15. *False.* Both of John's parents (and John) were of the priestly tribe of Levi (Luke 1:5). But Jesus was born of the kingly tribe of Judah (Matt. 1:2). In order to keep the tribes identifiable, mixed marriages were rare. Therefore John and Jesus were not related. "Cousin" in Luke 1:36 in the Greek *(suggenes)* actually means *countryman.*

16. *False.* John did not know Jesus, according to John 1:32-33.

17. *True.* The Bible says Mary wrapped Jesus in swaddling clothes (Luke 2:7). Ezek. 16:4 describes this Hebrew custom of cutting the navel, washing the infant's body, then salting it (probably to toughen the skin) and wrapping it in long strips of swaddling cloth, pinning the child's arms to his body so he can't scratch himself. Such practice was common in England a century ago.

18. *False.* The promised land, land of milk and honey, God's land (Lev. 25:23), was called *Canaan* during the days of the patriarchs Abraham, Isaac, and Jacob (2000 B.C.). Jacob's name was changed to Israel. The descendants of his twelve children, 600 years later, returned to the land from Egyptian bondage (the Exodus) and began calling the land *Israel.* Shortly after 1000 B.C. a great civil war divided the land. The northern kingdom took the name

Israel, and the southern kingdom, including Jerusalem, took the name Judah, after one of the tribes or sons of Jacob. When Israel was destroyed and Judah carried away in the Babylonian captivity (650 B.C.), the captives were called "Jews," because they were from Judah. When they returned home (500 B.C.), they called their land *Judea*, the Greek form of Judah. The land was called Judea during Jesus' lifetime. The Bible never uses the word *Palestine*, a name derived from Philistine, officially instituted in A.D. 136. The shape and size of this promised land is roughly the equivalent of New Hampshire. It is also interesting to note that *Hebrews* are descendants of Abraham, *Israelites* are descendants of Abraham's grandson Jacob, and *Jews* are descendants of Jacob's son Judah.

19. *False.* If you had shouted the name *Jesus* on the streets of Capernaum or Jerusalem in the days of our Lord, no one would have answered. In Exod. 6:3 God said His name is Jehovah (actually YHWH, expanded to Yahweh then Jehovah). The name Hosea means "salvation." By combining these two names, Jehovah and Hosea, we get *Jehoshua* or *Yehoshua*, meaning "Salvation God." Jesus is our Salvation God. These two names were shortened to *Joshua* and *Yeshua*. The Old Testament Joshua and Jesus actually had the same names. Joshua delivered Israel into the land of milk and honey. This person and historical event is a type that points to Jesus (same name), who delivers mankind into heaven (same event). The Old Testament was written in Hebrew, thus we read *Joshua*. The New Testament was written in Greek, and it reads *Iesous* (pronounced ee-ā-soos), the Greek form of Yeshua. Therefore we have the following names which apply to Jesus: Johoshua, Yehoshua, Joshua, Yeshua, Iesous, and as our Spanish-speaking neighbors pronounce it today,

"Hey-soose." Jesus' common language was Aramaic, a dialect of Hebrew. On the streets of Capernaum and Jerusalem, he was called *Yeshua*. Modern Hebrew places the emphasis upon the middle syllable, but in Jesus' day it was likely on the first. The familiar sound Jesus heard when someone called Him was *Yeshua* pronounced *Yes'-you-ah*.

20. *True.* Jesus spoke at least four languages: Aramaic, His everyday language; Hebrew, the language of the synagogue (Luke 4:16-20); Greek, the common language of the Gentiles, to whom Jesus preached without an interpreter; and Latin, the language of Rome and Pontius Pilate, to whom Jesus also spoke without an interpreter.

21. *True.* There is no mention of Joseph after Jesus began His ministry "at about thirty years of age" (Luke 3:23). Mary seems to have been alone, with Jesus the head of the family. Hanging upon the cross, Jesus asked His disciple John to look after the affairs of His mother (John 19:26-27).

22. Odd as it sounds, it is *true.* On the forty-first day after the birth of a boy child, the mother and the infant entered the Temple in Jerusalem for two purposes. First, the mother offered a lamb or a pair of turtledoves, the priest made an atonement, and the mother was made clean (Lev. 12:1-6). The second purpose called for a redemption (buying back) of the child. When God slew all the Egyptian firstborn sons at the great Exodus, He claimed for himself all the firstborn of Israel (Num. 3:12-13). Then He told the Israelites that only the descendants of Levi (Levites) were to be priests and all other firstborns were to be redeemed for five shekels (about $3.25, based on pre-1965 silver prices). Jesus was born of the tribe of Judah, not Levi. When He was brought to the Temple on

the forty-first day of His birth, Mary, a representative of the human race, bought Jesus from God for $3.25. How interesting to note that Judas Iscariot, another representative of the human race, sold Jesus over to Satanic forces for $19.50 (thirty pieces of silver), for a net profit of $16.25. How quick man is to respond to a material gain without weighing the true value of that which he is willing to surrender.

23. *True.* The distance from Nazareth in Galilee to Bethlehem in Judea is about 80 miles. If Joseph and Mary traveled the safer, more common route east of the Jordan River, it would have been about 100 miles. Travel was by foot and on the backs of donkeys or camels.

24. *False.* Much controversy and speculation surrounds this mystery. Over 100 different dates have been ascribed to Jesus' birth. Many say shepherds do not allow their flocks in the fields between November and April—too cold. Therefore Jesus was born in the summer or fall. But at the Florida-Georgia border (same latitude as Bethlehem) animals are kept out in December. Others say December 25 was selected in the fourth century by the Christian church, because on this longest night of the year pagans celebrated the victory of the god of light over the god of darkness. A competitive celebration was set up, a Christ Mass, to honor the birth of the "Light of the world." Josephus says Herod the Great died in March, 4 B.C. Sometime before this date Jesus was born, days later was taken to the Temple by His mother, and was visited by the wise men still later. Then came Herod's decree and the flight to Egypt, which lasted just a short time until Herod died. How long would all this take? About three months at the shortest. This places Jesus' birth in December of 5 B.C., a date accepted by many scholars. All

agree that the sixth-century Roman monk Dionysius Exiguus, who established the Christian calendar, miscalculated the birth year of Christ when he called it the year 0.

25. *False.* Mark and John begin their story at Jesus' baptism, when He was about thirty years old. Only Matthew and Luke tell the Christmas story. Matthew tells about the visit of the wise men; Luke tells of the shepherds. And only Luke tells of the actual birth. Only Matthew gives an account of the flight into Egypt and Herod's murder of the innocent children. Matthew met Jesus two years before the crucifixion and probably got his story from Jesus and His mother. Luke never met Jesus, but he researched his Gospel and got details of the birth from Mary, who surely remembered them well. Luke gives the most details, but both Matthew and Luke must be read for a complete story. Read from Matt. 1:18 to the end of chapter 2, comparing it to Luke 1:4-2:40.

How well did you do on your quiz? The important lesson from this chapter is that to know Jesus, we must turn to the Bible and read carefully and prayerfully. It is so easy for speculation and distortion to creep into our Christian doctrine if we rely solely upon outside sources.

10

*What would happen to Christianity if we acciden-
tally discovered all the lost writings of a religious
commune that existed near Jerusalem in the days
of Christ? We did, and speculation flourished concerning . . .*

Jesus and the Dead Sea Scrolls

In the spring of 1947, an Arab lad herding his flock in
the wilderness area on the northwest corner of the Dead
Sea hurled a stone into one of many narrow cave
openings dotting the hillside. He was startled by the
clunk of shattered clay. This young boy's find eventually
led to a mass excavation unearthing at least 400 manuscripts from eleven caves, a cemetery containing 1200
men and six women, and the ruins of Qumran. Qumran
was a community that began around 150 B.C. and was
destroyed by the Roman Tenth Legion that invaded
Israel and dispersed the Jews in A.D. 70, just forty years
after Jesus prophesied its destruction so profoundly
from the Mount of Olives on Palm Sunday (Luke 19:43-
44). The writers of the scrolls were Essenes, a Jewish
religious sect.

According to the Jewish historian Josephus, a resident
in or near the community for three years, there were
three sects of Judaism in his (and Jesus') day: Sadducees,
a liberal group mentioned fourteen times in the New
Testament; Pharisees, a conservative group mentioned
ninety-eight times; and Essenes, a socialist group not
once mentioned in the Christian Bible or Jewish Talmud.

99

It is believed Essenism, a blend of Judaism and Christian thought, was suppressed by each group because it contained elements of the other.

Information concerning the Essenes is found in writings of three first-century authors living during the period of Essene existence. The historians are Josephus (A.D. 37-95), born in Jerusalem just fifteen miles from Qumran; Philo (? B.C.-A.D. 50), born in Alexandria, Egypt, where he spent most of his life, perhaps 200 miles from Qumran but very near an Alexandrian branch of Essenes; and Pliny (A.D. 23-79), a Latin writer from Rome. From these historians we have the following information:

The Essenes

The Essenes, a religious sect (perhaps several thousand strong) dedicated to holiness, lived in large societies located throughout Israel and surrounding countries. The sect began under a still-unknown Teacher of Righteousness (who lived before Jesus was born) who probably left Jerusalem to form a group in Damascus. Eventually the group divided and reformed as individual communes throughout the land. No Essene strived for private property; material possessions were cast into a common pool supplying the wants of all. Neither poverty nor wealth existed.

The Essenes in most communities were celibate. They lived without women, considering all forms of sexual intercourse sinful. Escapees from the busy, competitive lifestyle in Judea continually replenished their ranks. Jews, tired and desiring to return to the simple lifestyle experienced by their ancestors in the forty-year wilderness wandering, resorted to an Essene community.

Each commune member served three years probation,

performing a job assigned according to his talents. Some tilled the soil, others tended the flocks, still others cared for beehives or rolled mud rooftops. Artisans and craftsmen anticipated the community needs and manufactured goods and wares. Each member worked with vigor, patience, and good cheer, never excusing himself during inclement weather. Their work, considered rigid gymnastics, was more productive than athletic. Here is a glimpse of a typical day at the Essene commune.

A Typical Day

The day begins before sunrise with meditation and prayer. Secular matters are rarely discussed—never before sunup. Dismissed by their task overseer, the members work until eleven A.M., reassemble, and dress in linen aprons to undergo a ritualistic bathing—a purification rite—a type of baptism. Next they uniformly gather in a large dining room from which strangers are excluded as if it is a sacred temple. In silence, they sit. The baker places a small bread loaf and the cook, a plate of vegetables, before every member. Each receives just enough to satisfy his needs. A priest says grace; they break fast.

After the silent meal, another prayer is offered. Then, white garments laid aside, they resume work until evening then return to eat supper with any visiting guests. Clothing is all alike: summer, a cheap, sleeveless tunic and winter, a thick cloak. Garments are hung in a common closet and selected at random. If any man falls sick, his care and recovery is the concern of all. Old men, childless, are honored and cared for by the community "children" as old-age welfare. Both citizen and king praise the fraternity for their dedication to the study of nature's great truths.

Qumran

The preceding description, capsuled from the writings of the three first-century historians is descriptive of Essenes in general, living throughout the land. The writers of the Dead Sea Scrolls belonged to one of these Essene communities, Qumran, resting on a flat hilltop about a quarter mile above the Dead Sea coast. Here, the homestead was composed of several stone hovels enclosed in a wall. There were kitchens, pantries for storing dried foods, a bakery, workshops for repairing tools, and kilns for heating large bricks. A few hundred yards behind Qumran are caves where many of its residents lived. An aqueduct ascending the eastern highlands delivered water to the rocky commune. A large vegetable farm, two miles south of Qumran, fed its few hundred inhabitants. The community was governed by twelve laymen and three priests.

Jesus and the Essenes

Jesus knew of the Essenes and their teaching, the eminence of the end of the age. While Christianity and Essenism developed from the same roots—the Old Testament (including its prophecies of a coming Messiah)—there were differences in beliefs. Jesus believed in living an abundant life, using oil to anoint the body, wholesomeness of marriage, bodily resurrection, eating meat, and doing good works on the Sabbath. The Essenes were ascetic abstainers, opposed to all these ideas. It is generally believed John the Baptist, an ascetic abstainer, was greatly influenced by the Essenes, possibly spending much time amongst them. The wilderness area where

John preached was the same vicinity as Qumran.

If Jesus' teachings (such as the Sermon on the Mount) have overtones of earlier Essene writings, it is because Jesus often used Old Testament and contemporary teachings of love, kindness, and virtue to relate truth and fullness of life. Some scholars claim Jesus was an Essene. Supportive evidence simply does not exist.

The Scrolls

The community's main function was performed in the scriptorium. Here, scribes religiously copied sacred Jewish scriptures, their own commentaries, apocalypses, and a *Manual of Discipline.* It was this scroll library that was placed in large, clay jars and hidden in caves around Qumran above the Dead Sea just before the destruction of the community in A.D. 70. The Essenes had planned to return to their ruined abode and hidden library after the heat of war settled down. They never returned. The scrolls remained hidden nearly 1900 years. The Essenes have disappeared, but we have their library of writings.

At the discovery of ancient manuscripts in caves above the Dead Sea in 1947 there came an era of eyebrow raising from concerned Christians. Would the new find change beliefs of traditional Christianity? Or worse, would it alter our sacred message of salvation?

Publishing companies quickly offered books and articles with such titles as *The Lost Years of Jesus, The Wilderness of John the Baptist Discovered,* and *Mysterious Scrolls Alter Christianity.* Theologians began long, intense studies to see how Christianity would be affected, if at all, by these scrolls. Years passed and now thousands of Christians who never read translations of the scrolls but remember those frightening book titles and reports still wonder. What did those scrolls say, anyhow? Here is what they said.

Old Testament Scrolls
Among the thousands of scroll fragments discovered, scholars have found excerpts of every book in the Old Testament except Esther. And in some cases (such as Isaiah), the entire book is intact. Secular scrolls unique to the Essene community were also found.

The Copper Scroll
Most of the scrolls found in the Dead Sea caves are printed on leather, some on the hair side. In 1952, two copper scrolls were found in cave number three. The two scrolls had originally been one, but an accident broke it in half. In 1956, *Time* magazine published a quote from the copper scroll describing the location of 600 bars of silver and a vessel of incense in pine and cassia wood. It remains a puzzle why an ascetic community abstaining from worldly riches would concern themselves with these mundane affairs.

Manual of Discipline
This leather scroll fragment is nine inches high and six feet long. It is considered to be the book of principles governing the community. In it we are given several names by which the community called itself (The Men of the Covenant, The Council or Party, The Community, and The Congregation) and names for its members (sons of righteousness, sons of light, sons of truth). Nonmembers too are given names (sons of perversion, sons of darkness, treacherous men, and men of the pit). From this scroll we also learn of the community's daily ceremonial bathings,

their communal meals, their high regard for the Jewish Scriptures (Old Testament), the democratic elements of their government, the council of twelve who had final authority, the abandonment of worldly goods and probation period of its new members, the rigorous discipline against slander, and their sacred claim, "All that is and ever was comes from the God of Knowledge."

Habakkuk Commentary

Habakkuk is an Old Testament book about a prophet who sees the oncoming destruction of Jerusalem by the wicked Babylonians in the sixth century B.C. and asks God "Why?" One of the Dead Sea Scrolls is a commentary on this book, claiming the enemy in verse 1:6 are the *kittim* or the Romans, not the ancient Babylonians. The Habakkuk interpreter predicts the oncoming destruction of Jerusalem by the Romans. In this scroll we read of the Teacher of Righteousness, the unnamed priest-leader of the community who supposedly knew "all the mysteries of the words of God's prophets," though he was not considered a prophet himself. We also learn of the Wicked Priest, who was evil and opposed to the community and was believed to have murdered the Teacher of Righteousness about a century before the birth of Jesus.

The Thanksgiving Scroll

This scroll is a collection of approximately thirty-five psalms, most beginning with "I thank thee, God" (hence, the assigned title). The psalms were written by an Israelite who possibly lived at the Qumran community where the scrolls were found. Many scholars believe the Teacher of Righteousness was the author. This conclusion is based on the statement, "They drive me from my land like a bird from its nest," found in the scroll. This statement parallels the Habakkuk Commentary account of the Wicked Priest driving the Teacher of Righteousness into exile. The style of the psalms imitates the biblical Psalms.

The War Scroll

Six inches high and over nine feet long, this scroll is in nearly perfect condition. It tells of a battle between the "Children of Light" and the "Children of Darkness." Scholars are not sure to which battle it refers. Many think of the wars of the Maccabees in 165 B.C., or the civil war in the time of Alexander Jannaeus in 90 B.C. Others believe it is a prediction of the war yet to occur, the one the Qumran community was expecting. Still others are sure it refers to a spiritual war between good and evil. The scroll identifies the Children of Light with Jews from the tribes of Judah, Levi, and Benjamin. The Children of Darkness are the troops from the land southeast of Judea across the Dead Sea and the troops southwest of Judea, in Philistia. The battle is not described, but victory is assured the Children of Light and, "There shall be no survivor of the Sons of Darkness." The battle seems to be one of great conflict and confrontation, yet with assured victory. This theme parallels the Bible that promises victory for believers in the midst of conflict and confrontation.

The Temple Scroll

A major portion of this scroll is comprised of instructions for Israel's defense against the enemy. Unlike the War Scroll that describes a spiritual, idealized battle, the Temple Scroll is more practical: 23,000 body guards to protect the king, one-fifth of the people to be drafted at the sound of war, one-half to actually engage in battle when the war begins, and so forth. About half of this scroll gives details for building and furnishing the Temple. The description is similar to that found in Exodus 35-40 concerning the Tabernacle.

The Genesis Apocryphon
This scroll was not opened until 1956 when it was purchased by the Israeli government. It contains a paraphrase of Genesis 5-15 in Aramaic and includes legends. There is a description of the topography in the land of Lot and expounds on Sarah's beauty.

The preceding evidence and the testimony of respected scholars give adequate indication that the Dead Sea Scrolls have not revolutionized traditional Christianity, nor changed any of its doctrine or beliefs. What the discovery of the scrolls has given us is a clearer picture of Essenes, the authors of the scrolls, and their beliefs; the importance of Judaism outside Pharisaic Jerusalem (Essenes did not use the Temple); life and language during the pre-Christian and early Christian era; and (perhaps) more knowledge of the early life and background of John the Baptist.

PART THREE

THOSE REMARKABLE
PROPHECIES

11

The claim that Jesus is the son of God is the most paradoxical claim in all the world. Nevertheless, the evidence for this claim is overwhelming. The amazing aspect of fulfilled prophecy is another piece of evidence that authenticates the Bible. Such as . . .

Thirty Prophecies Fulfilled in Twenty-Four Hours

If I had to go to court as defense attorney to prove to the world that Jesus is the Messiah, I could roll in a wheelbarrow full of evidence. But I wouldn't. I would take just one history book—the Bible. To me it is the inspired word of God, exposing the truth about life that sets people free. But to the court it would be just a history book entered as evidence. I would tell the court that the authors who penned the Old Testament made hundreds of predictions about this man Jesus *long before He was born*. They wrote about His virgin birth (Isa. 7:14), about the town He was to be born in (Mic. 5:2), who His ancestors would be (Gen. 22:18), that He would ride into Jerusalem on a donkey's back (Zech. 9:9). As a matter of fact, all of history focused on this person who was yet to be born.

And every prediction came true—*exactly as predicted*.

Then the court would ask to see some of these miraculous predictions as evidence.

My examples would come from the last twenty-four hours before the stone was rolled over Jesus' tomb. That is, the events that occurred from 6:00 P.M. Thursday,

April 6, A.D. 30 to 6:00 P.M. Friday, April 7. During this time Jesus had His Last Supper with His disciples, prayed at Gethsemane, stood trial throughout the night, and was crucified. Here is what these historians said about this last day. (They spoke in the present tense because in the spiritual realm *all* is eternity—there is no past or future; everything is *now*.)

Betrayed by a Friend

Over a thousand years before Jesus was born, King David received word that his dear friend and chief counselor, Ahithophel, had turned against him: "And one told David, saying, Ahithophel is among the conspirators with Absalom" (2 Sam. 15:31). In despair, David sat down and wrote Psalm 55. And as so often happened when David, the anointed one of God, reached deep into his soul to solidify his feelings, he disclosed an element of reality that belonged to another world—the world of Jesus, the promised Messiah. David prophetically sang:

> For it was not an enemy that reproached me; then I could have borne it: neither was it he that hated me that did magnify himself against me; then I would have hid myself from him: But it was thou, a man mine equal, my guide, and mine acquaintance. We took sweet counsel together, and walked unto the house of God in company. (Ps. 55:12-14)

As is so frequently in the case of prophecy, there are two meanings, two interpretations: one local and current, one reaching forward in time to reveal truth. While David, locally and currently, sang of the conspiracy of his friend, a thousand years later we find this prophetic utterance illuminating and documenting reality in the

112

life of Christ. This prophecy went forth and found its mark in the events recorded in John 13:21-22.

When Jesus had thus said, he was troubled in spirit, and testified, and said, Verily, verily, I say unto you, that one of you shall betray me.

It was not an enemy who reproached Jesus. Neither was it one who hated Him. It was His acquaintance, and together they had walked into the house of God.

The relationship of David and Ahithophel is very similar to that of Jesus and His betrayer, Judas; just as Ahithophel committed suicide by hanging himself (2 Sam. 17:23), so did Judas (Matt. 27:5).

Documented evidence in the form of fulfilled prophecy in the life of Christ is abundant. See what else the Scriptures foretold about this betrayer-friend.

In Psalm 41 David sings:

Yea, mine own familiar friend, in whom I trusted, which did eat of my bread, hath lifted up his heel against me. (verse 9)

John the Apostle, recording the events of Jesus' Last Supper hundreds of years later, wrote:

Jesus answered, He it is, to whom I shall give a sop, when I have dipped it. And when he had dipped the sop, he gave it to Judas Iscariot, the son of Simon. (John 13:26)

The sop refers to a portion of the Passover meal Jesus was taking, a morsel of lamb wrapped in unleavened bread and dipped in a bitter herb sauce, then handed to the guest of honor to take the first bite. Many in the world still "sop" gravy or sauce with some form of bread.

Jesus was honoring His familiar friend whom He trusted, "which did eat of my bread." Again, David's prophecy finds its mark in the promised Messiah a thousand years after its utterance.

Now see what the prophet Zechariah stated in 487 B.C. concerning this event.

And I said unto them, If ye think good, give me my price; and if not, forbear. So they weighed for my price thirty pieces of silver. And the Lord said unto me, Cast it unto the potter. (Zech. 11:12-13)

Yet another proclamation of God concerning an event that was not to occur for 500 years—the betrayal of Jesus for a mere thirty pieces of silver. The prophecy finds its mark in the events of Matt. 27:9-10, where it states:

And they took the thirty pieces of silver, the price of him that was valued, whom they of the children of Israel did value; and gave them for the potter's field, as the Lord appointed me.

Arrest in Gethsemane

After supper Jesus and His friends sang a hymn and walked north along the Kidron Brook to the Garden of Gethsemane on the Mount of Olives bordering Jerusalem. Concerning these few hours of prayer and arrest our historian-prophets wrote:

They that hate me without a cause are more than the hairs of mine head. (Ps. 69:4)

Jesus is the only man who could ever be hated "without a cause," for He is the only man who ever lived without sin (Rom. 3:23). Was Jesus really hated? Read His own words.

But now have they both seen and hated both me and
my Father. (John 15:24)

Who were those that hated Jesus—the common community? No, for they had greeted Him with shouts and
praise and the waving of palm fronds a few days earlier
as He rode into Jerusalem (Matt. 21:8-11). See who the
ancient prophets claimed would hate Him.

The kings of the earth set themselves, and the rulers
take counsel together, against the Lord, and against
his anointed. (Ps. 2:2)

The Lord and the anointed, as David wrote, were God
and King David, the author of this psalm. But David was
also a prophet, and this prophetic utterance found its
mark in Jesus, the anointed of the Lord (How many years
later?).

And they that had laid hold on Jesus led him away to
Caiaphas the high priest, where the scribes and the
elders were assembled. (Matt. 26:57)

The high priest, scribes, and elders were the rulers of
Palestine. Pontius Pilate's authority was supported by
the king of the land, Tiberius Caesar (Luke 3:1).
When Jesus was arrested, it is recorded that His disciples deserted Him.

Then all the disciples forsook him, and fled. (Matt.
26:56)

But wasn't this also predicted in the sacred history of
the Jews—500 years before it occurred?

Awake, O sword, against my shepherd, and against the man that is my fellow, saith the Lord of hosts: smite the shepherd, and the sheep shall be scattered. (Zech. 13:7)

The Trials Begin

At midnight, Jesus was taken to trial before the Sanhedrin (Jewish court), then to Herod, and shortly after sunrise, to Pontius Pilate. He underwent six trials throughout the long and sad night. Here is what our historian-prophets foretold would occur during the trials: Jesus would stand silent before His accusers.

He was oppressed, and he was afflicted, yet he opened not his mouth: he is brought as a lamb to the slaughter, and as a sheep before her shearers is dumb, so he openeth not his mouth. (Isa. 53:7)

Isaiah wrote 700 years before the birth of Jesus. His prophecies about Jesus are many. This one finds its mark in Matthew.

And when he was accused of the chief priests and elders, he answered nothing. (Matt. 27:12)

The prophet Micah in the same decade prophesied Jesus would be struck with a rod.

They shall smite the judge of Israel with a rod upon the cheek. (Mic. 5:1)

The fulfillment of this prophecy is recorded in the New Testament book of Matthew.

And they . . . took the reed, and smote him on the head. (Matt. 27:30)

116

The Old Testament further says:

False witnesses are risen up against me. (Ps. 27:12)

And the New Testament certifies:

Now the chief priests, and elders, and all the council, sought false witness against Jesus, to put him to death. (Matt. 26:59)

Then the Old Testament vows Jesus will be despised and abhorred.

Thus saith the Lord, the Redeemer of Israel, and his Holy One, to him whom man despiseth, to him whom the nation abhorreth. (Isa. 49:7)

And the New Testament shows this to be true.

Pilate saith unto them, What shall I do then with Jesus which is called Christ? They all say unto him, Let him be crucified. (Matt. 27:22)

The Old Testament pronounces:

I gave my back to the smiters. (Isa. 50:6)

And the New Testament echoes:

Then Pilate therefore took Jesus, and scourged [whipped] him. (John 19:1)

The Old Testament declares they would strike Him with their hands until He is hardly recognizable.

As many were astonied at thee; his visage [face] was so marred more than any man, and his form more than the sons of men. (Isa. 52:14)

And the New Testament confirms:

And others smote him with the palms of their hands.
(Matt. 26:67)

What a dark night it was for mankind. The Creator of
the universe was despised, struck in the face with a rod
of reed, whipped until blood spilled from His back, and
struck in the face with bare hands. It was even prophesied they would spit upon Him; men spat upon the one
who had come to die for them.

I hid not my face from shame and spitting. (Isa. 50:6)

The New Testament authenticates the prophecy.

Then did they spit in his face, and buffeted him.
(Matt. 26:67)

Jesus was alone in the large chambers as dozens of men
cursed Him, mocked Him, and pulled hair from His beard
(Isa. 50:6), while hundreds outside shouted, "Crucify
him, crucify him!"
The whole story was told by God through His prophets
long before it happened. And why did it have to happen?
God told us that also.

He was wounded for our transgressions, he was
bruised for our iniquities: the chastisement of our
peace was upon him; and with his stripes we are
healed. (Isa. 53:5)

Jesus suffered so that we might be healed—our spirits
and our bodies. He was sacrificed as a lamb upon an altar
so that we might have eternal life. He was the Lamb of
God about to go to the cross. As He was being whipped
(His stripes), we were being healed.

The Crucifixion

At 9:00 A.M. Jesus was sentenced by the Roman government, under much pressure from the Jews. He was taken to the cross to be crucified. Again the Old Testament resounds across the ages with minute details of what was about to occur.

They pierced my hands and my feet. (Ps. 22:16)

This song of David was written a thousand years before Christ, long before crucifixion was used as a means of execution. When David pronounced these words, the sound of his voice may have been audibly heard only a few feet away, but the voice went on, crossing the hills of southern Judah and penetrating the sky above in an ever-increasing concentric sphere, racing across time and the universe, resounding throughout all of heaven, "they pierced my hands and my feet."

Five hundred years later the message was repeated. Even God has reruns of the important events of life.

And one shall say unto him, What are these wounds in thine hands? Then he shall answer, Those with which I was wounded in the house of my friends. (Zech. 13:6)

And in another 500 years, Dr. Luke, the Greek physician, documented it.

And when they were come to the place, which is called Calvary, there they crucified him. (Luke 23:33)

Here now are some of the details of the crucifixion prophesied in the Old Testament and fulfilled in the New Testament.

	Old Testament	New Testament
• Jesus will pray for those who crucify him.	Isa. 53:12	Luke 23:34
• They will cast lots for his coat and divide his garment.	Ps. 22:18	John 19:23
• He will be given gall for food.	Ps. 69:21	Matt. 27:34
• His bones will be pulled out of joint (a result of hanging on the cross).	Ps. 22:14	Luke 23:33
• He will cry out to God, "Why hast thou forsaken me?"	Ps. 22:1	Matt. 27:46
• His friends will watch from afar off.	Ps. 38:11	Luke 24:49
• He will become very thirsty.	Ps. 22:15	John 19:28
• He will be poured out like water.	Ps. 22:14	John 19:34
• No bone in his body will be broken.	Ps. 34:20	John 19:32-36
• He will be encircled by Romans (dogs).	Ps. 22:16	Matt. 27:36
• He will give up his spirit to God.	Ps. 31:5	Luke 23:46
• He will die along with criminals.	Isa. 53:9	Mark 15:27
• He will be buried in a rich man's tomb.	Isa. 53:9	Matt. 27:57-60
• He will die having no deceit or violence in his life.	Isa. 53:9	1 Pet. 2:22

Verdict Please

Remarkable! Thirty details of the events surrounding the last twenty-four hours before Jesus entered the tomb a deceased *but not defeated* man. And all of them written years before they occurred—written, documented, and protected as sacred by a nation of people who knew God intimately.

What are the chances of all thirty events occurring as predicted? A mathematician would say one chance in 1,073,741,824 (two to the thirtieth power). The chances of all thirty prophecies being fulfilled is a billion to one. Couple these odds to the chance that hundreds of years later all thirty prophecies would be fulfilled in a *single twenty-four-hour period*, and the mathematical ratio becomes infinitesimal.

If the thought has ever entered your mind that maybe these prophecies were not telling about Jesus, read all of Isaiah 53 and all of Psalm 22 in the Old Testament. It will give you chills.

Even the Jew who reads these accounts of *his* history must join with the Roman soldier who stood before the cross and saw it all and concluded, "Truly this man was the Son of God" (Mark 15:39).

12

If the Bible is from God and tells the entire history of man on earth, shouldn't we expect to find hints of God's greatest gift to man in every book, beginning with the very first?

Jesus in the Ancient Book of Genesis

Where else but in the record of the beginning of all earthly things, Genesis, is there a better place to introduce Jesus? But let us remember that Jesus existed even before this. Jesus has always been in existence.

In the beginning was the Word, and the Word was with God, and the Word was God. The same was in the beginning with God. (John 1:1-2)

The *Word* is capitalized; it refers to a divine Person. This Person existed from the very beginning, long before the earth was created, and He was with God and in fact *was* God. That the *Word* is Jesus is proven by the following Scriptures.

And the Word was made flesh, and dwelt among us, (and we beheld his glory, the glory as of the only begotten of the Father,) full of grace and truth. (John 1:14)

And he was clothed with a vesture dipped in blood: and his name is called the Word of God. (Rev. 19:13)

In the renowned Micah prophecy that names the exact town wherein Jesus was to be born we also read of his preexistence.

But thou, Bethlehem Ephratah, though thou be little among the thousands of Judah, yet out of thee shall he come forth unto me that is to be ruler in Israel; whose goings forth have been from old, from everlasting. (Mic. 5:2)

Not only did Jesus exist from the very beginning, He *is* the beginning, as we see when he describes himself as the first and last letter of the Greek alphabet.

I am Alpha and Omega, the beginning and the ending, saith the Lord, which is, and which was, and which is to come, the Almighty. (Rev. 1:8)

About two thousand years ago Jesus took on a fleshly form, in order to present himself as the ultimate sacrifice to atone for the sin that had come into the world and diseased God's people. That we might understand this intricate process and accept Jesus as the Christ—and be granted abundant life on earth and eternal fellowship after life—is the full purpose of the Bible.

I am come that they might have life, and that they might have it more abundantly. (John 10:10)

Whosoever believeth in him should not perish, but have everlasting life. (John 3:16)

And many other signs truly did Jesus in the presence of his disciples, which are not written in this book: But these are written, that ye might believe that Jesus is the Christ, the Son of God; and that believing ye might have life through his name. (John 20:30-31)

On many Bibles there is a red thread hanging from the

binding, used to mark the place of the reader. This thread is a tangible symbol of an intangible red thread that weaves through every book in the Bible. It is the thread of truth, the thread of salvation; it is the trail of the atoning blood of Jesus. In every book of the Bible there is some hint or symbol that tells the greatest story of all, the story of the Son of God, whose blood was sacrificially spilled so that mankind might be saved from eternal destruction. This thread begins in the book of Genesis.

When we want our children to learn the intricate concepts of physics and higher mathematics, we begin by teaching them one plus one equals two. God introduces the virgin birth, the need for Jesus to lose blood on the cross, and other complex biblical concepts very slowly also, by creating simple worldly parallels. As mentioned earlier, these parallel situations or objects are called *types*. Here are six types of Jesus from the book of Genesis that God has given us to study and understand.

Jesus—the Seed of Woman (Gen. 3:15)

In the Garden of Eden, the serpent (Satan) convinced Eve to eat of the forbidden tree of knowledge. Punishment for disobeying God included a prophetic utterance to the serpent that reads, "And I will put enmity between thee and the woman, and between thy seed and her seed" (Gen. 3:15). In other words, Satan and the seed of woman will forever be enemies.

Now, as we know, all flesh is born of the seed of man. It is man's seed planted in the womb of woman that effects reproduction. But here God says the opposing force against Satan will be born of the seed of woman. Only once in the history of the world has this occurred—when Jesus was born of the virgin Mary. This biological process is called *parthenogenesis* and is common in certain lower forms of plant and insect life. Parthenogenetic (seedless) grapes are not uncommon. Parthenogenesis is reproduction by the development of an unfertilized ovum and has never occurred in humans except in the case of Mary.

Exactly what process God used we cannot know. With certain fruits, a mechanical or chemical process is used to develop the virgin-born fruit. In the unique and necessary case of Mary, the Bible says it was caused by action of the Holy Spirit.

> Then said Mary unto the angel, How shall this be, seeing I know not a man? And the angel answered and said unto her, The Holy Ghost shall come upon thee, and the power of the Highest shall overshadow thee: therefore also that holy thing which shall be born of thee shall be called the Son of God. (Luke 1:34-35)

In a most subtle manner, right at the beginning of His book to mankind, God introduces Jesus as the soon-to-come, virgin-born archenemy of Satan.

Jesus—the Coat of Skin (Gen. 3:21)

As a result of Adam and Eve's disobedience in the Garden, their eyes were opened to their nakedness, and they felt shame for the first time. In order to cover this shame, they made clothes of fig leaves.

> And the eyes of them both were opened, and they knew that they were naked; and they sewed fig leaves together, and made themselves aprons. (Gen. 3:7)

But reading on, we see that God did not honor the clothes made from plant life as an adequate material to cover their shame, a result of their disobedience. Instead God gave them coats made of animal skins.

Unto Adam also and to his wife did the Lord God make coats of skins, and clothed them. (Gen. 3:21)

Who killed the animals to make the coats? God did. God had to sacrifice an animal, spill his blood, in order to make those coats to cover the shame of His children. The fig leaves would not do. God was saying *blood must be spilled* to cover sin. God ordained the sacrificial system used throughout the Old Testament so that when he sent His Son Jesus to shed blood on the cross we would understand why. Jesus *has* shed His blood and become the coat that covers sin and shame and removes guilt from all who are willing to accept Him as Savior.

Jesus—Abel's Animal Sacrifice (Gen. 4:3-5)

To further support the necessity of spilling blood, we read in Gen. 4:3-5 that when Cain sacrificed some of the plants from his garden, God would not accept the sacrifice (no blood spilled). But when Abel offered the animals from his flock, God respected it.

And in process of time it came to pass, that Cain brought of the fruit of the ground an offering unto the Lord. And Abel, he also brought of the firstlings of his flock and of the fat thereof. And the Lord had respect unto Abel and to his offering: But unto Cain and to his offering he had not respect. And Cain was very much wroth, and his countenance fell.

Again God reemphasizes the fact that if the sacrificial

127

offering is to be good, blood must be spilled.

> By faith Abel offered unto God a more excellent sacrifice than Cain, by which he obtained witness that he was righteous, God testifying of his gifts: and by it he being dead yet speaketh. (Heb. 11:4)

The Bible says that Cain was rejected because there was no faith in his sacrifice; his spirit was on the wrong track. But it also says, "and to his offering he had not respect." The offering itself was the wrong kind.

> And almost all things are by the law purged with blood; and without shedding of blood is no remission. (Heb. 9:22)

Why God chose the spilling of blood to atone for sin I do not know. If I had been in charge of creating this world, I probably would have selected another means. But I wasn't in charge, God was. I am very small and of limited intelligence; God is neither small nor limited. God chose the sacrificial system; let us accept it.

But we must remember that Abel's sacrifice, as well as the subsequent blood sacrifices under Mosaic law, were signs of the ultimate sacrifice, Jesus. And after Jesus, the sacrificial system was replaced by the sacramental system: Baptism, the symbolic dipping of a believer into the blood of Christ; and Holy Communion, the symbolic drinking of the blood of Christ. Through these two sacraments, the body of the believer becomes symbolically saturated in the atoning blood of Christ, both inside and out.

Both these sacraments are made valid by the remembering and the faith that Cain lacked. We indulge and partake and remember the ultimate sacrifice, Jesus. No longer is blood spilling necessary; Jesus did it all. Now he asks us to use Baptism and Holy Communion to help us remember the blood-streaked lashes on his back: "and with his stripes we are healed" (Isa. 53:5), and the blood that spilled from his body when the crown of thorns was pushed into his forehead, when spikes were driven into his hands and feet, when a spear was thrust into his heart.

For if the blood of bulls and of goats, and the ashes of an heifer sprinkling the unclean, sanctifieth to the purifying of the flesh: How much more shall the blood of Christ, who through the eternal Spirit offered himself without spot to God, purge your conscience from dead works to serve the living God? (Heb. 9:13-14)

Now we know why so many Christian groups today emphasize the blood. They are not vampires; they simply understand that we are freed from sin because Jesus spilled His blood on the cross. It was not His virgin birth, His sinless life, nor his resurrected body that removed the deadly death venom from our bloodline; it was His *spilled blood.*

Abel's blood-spilling sacrifice in Genesis is a prelude to the blood that stained the old rugged cross; the first blood offering points to the last. With the acceptance of Abel's animal sacrifice God is saying, "This is the way it is going to be with my Son when He comes; His blood will be spilled as the ultimate sacrifice to set mankind free."

Jesus—the Ark of Salvation (Gen. 7:1, 7)
It was through faith that Noah built and entered the

ark of safety. He was warned of things not yet seen. His tireless construction of the ark before a ridiculing crowd became the evidence of his faith, "the evidence of things not seen" (Heb. 11:1).

> By faith Noah, being warned of God of things not seen as yet, moved with fear, prepared an ark to the saving of his house; by the which he condemned the world, and became heir of the righteousness which is by faith. (Heb. 11:7)

It is through an application of this same faith that we must enter the body of Christ, our ark of salvation. We too are warned of things unseen—eternal damnation— the same condemnation received by those who did not enter Noah's ark. But by entering into fellowship with Jesus, we float above the turbulent waters of condemnation.

> There is therefore now no condemnation to them which are in Christ Jesus, who walk not after the flesh, but after the spirit. (Rom. 8:1)

The flood waters of Noah's day represent the wrath of God poured upon unbelievers. It is the condemnation from which no unbeliever can escape. The ark is Jesus, the only hope. Noah and his family represent the believers of the world, the Christians.

> And the Lord said unto Noah, Come thou and all thy house into the ark; for thee have I seen righteous before me in this generation. (Gen. 7:1)

God speaks to each of us and simply says, "I have warned you of things unseen, and I have provided an ark of safety, Jesus. Now enter in."

And Noah went in, and his sons, and his wife, and his sons' wives with him, into the ark, because of the waters of the flood. (Gen. 7:7)

God could have chosen many ways to destroy the sinful race that existed in Noah's day. He could have used fire, or an epidemic disease, or any of several natural disasters. He could have even used a miraculous unnatural disaster. But he chose instead a means that would best express man's relationship to Christ and the world. He wanted us to see the continued faith of Noah as he built a huge ark month after month in a high and dry land. He wanted to express the condemnation poured upon sinful mankind day after day, night after night, a condemnation so vast it permeates every crevice. He shows us that those who enter into fellowship with Jesus will be saved, but it is important to see the only ones allowed to enter are those who believe and show their faith. God doesn't want us to wait until our dying day to accept His Son. He wants us to believe now. If there are no believers *before the flood*, there are no workers, no one to build the ark.

The entire event, from the securing of the first log to the resting of the ark on Mt. Ararat, took many months, perhaps years. It was a slow, determined process whereby each phase could be studied. God wanted us to see Jesus, the Ark of our salvation, and to understand what is required, if we are to avoid condemnation. Enter in.

Jesus—the Sacrificed Isaac (Gen. 22)
The twenty-second chapter of Genesis tells the story of Abraham, who, in obedience to God, offered his son Isaac as a human sacrifice. The whole ordeal is a picture-

prophecy of the death and resurrection of Christ.

Again God is preparing a nation (Israel), and all who read this Scripture, to accept and understand the ultimate event of the human race, the bodily resurrection of a human being. God wants us to know it really happened. He hints of the event time and again. He wants us to be assured it will happen to us—bodily resurrection, the Christian hope.

> And it came to pass after these things, that God did tempt Abraham, and said unto him, Abraham: and he said, Behold, here I am. And he said, Take now thy son, thine only son Isaac, whom thou lovest, and get thee into the land of Moriah; and offer him there for a burnt offering upon one of the mountains which I will tell thee of. (Gen. 22:1-2)

Notice how God emphasizes *thine only son* to remind us later of Jesus, His *only son.* And He sent them to the land of Moriah, which is Jerusalem and its environs, the same area in which Jesus was delivered for the crucifixion. Abraham's *only son* is to be offered as a *sacrifice* in *Jerusalem*—sound familiar?

> And Abraham rose up early in the morning, and saddled his ass, and took two of his young men with him, and Isaac his son. (Gen. 22:3)

Accompanying Isaac to his sacrificial death were two young men, Isaac's contemporaries. Are you reminded that when Jesus went to his sacrificial death, two contemporaries hung at his side?

> Then on the third day Abraham lifted up his eyes, and saw the place afar off. (Gen. 22:4)

It was the third day after Abraham received word that his son must be offered that they came to the hill which God had selected. We are never told which hill, but many today believe it was Mt. Calvary, the highest hill in Jerusalem, the one upon which Christ gave his blood.

For three days Isaac was considered dead by Abraham, as he prepared to obey God's order to sacrifice him. Likewise Jesus was considered dead as his body lay in the tomb for three days.

And Abraham said unto his young men, Abide ye here with the ass; and I and the lad will go yonder and worship, and come again to you. (Gen. 22:5)

This aspect of the event foreshadows Jesus entering deep into Gethsemane to pray. Abraham represents God and Isaac, Jesus. The two are alone to pray before the sacrificial death, while the companions are left to wait.

When Jesus was in the garden with God in prayer before his sacrificial death, he also left his companions to wait at a distance.

And Abraham took the wood of the burnt offering, and laid it upon Isaac his son. (Gen. 22:6)

Just as Jesus had to carry his own cross upon his shoulders, Isaac had to carry upon his shoulders the wood that was to destroy his body.

The story goes on to tell that as Abraham was about to slay his son upon the altar and burn his body, he was stopped by an angel, and a ram was provided by God to replace Isaac. God never meant for any man other than His own Son to be sacrificed. Cults believing otherwise are surely doomed to eternal condemnation.

This entire event, directed by God, was simply a test of

Abraham's faith—"for now I know that thou fearest God" (Gen. 22:12)—and a figurative model of the death and resurrection of Jesus. Read how it was described in a letter to the Hebrews some 2000 years later:

> By faith Abraham, when he was tried, offered up Isaac. . . Accounting that God was able to raise him up, even from the dead; from whence also he received him in a figure. (Heb. 11:17-19)

On the third day, God returned Abraham's only son, the son of promise. (Ishmael, Abraham's previous son by a slave girl, was gone, and his other sons were not yet born; thus Isaac became his only son.) Can you imagine the joy felt by Abraham when God *figuratively* raised him from the dead? Can you imagine the joy felt by the world (to whom Jesus was dead for three days) when God *literally* raised Jesus from the dead? Clearly, in the events of the sacrificed Isaac, God reveals another segment in the life of His Son, Jesus.

Jesus—the Exalted Joseph (Gen. 37)
When Isaac grew up, he had a son named Jacob, later renamed Israel. Jacob had twelve sons, and each became the head of an Israelite tribe, thus forming the twelve tribes of Israel.

In Genesis 37 we begin reading of the life of Joseph, the most favored of the twelve sons. Right away we notice that Joseph, like Isaac, is a type of Jesus, another example offered by God to prove to the Israelites and all the world that Jesus is the promised Messiah.

Like Jesus, Joseph was a very special son. Jacob "loved Joseph more than all his children" (37:3). As a result of this, a relationship evolved between Joseph and his brothers that reminds us of the relationship that was to exist at a much later date between Jesus and the Jews of his day, a relationship of hatred, jealousy, and envy because the father showed special favor. In Joseph's case, his father "made him a coat of many colors" (37:3). In Jesus' case his father clothed him with many colorful talents: miracle-working abilities, wisdom, great teaching tactics, perseverance, patience, strength.

And when his brethren saw that their father loved him more than all his brethren, they hated him, and could not speak peaceably unto him. (Gen. 37:4)

Like Joseph, Jesus also became the hated one. Then Joseph had two dreams:

For, behold, we were binding sheaves in the field, and, lo, my sheaf arose, and also stood upright; and, behold, your sheaves stood round about, and made obeisance to my sheaf. And his brethren said to him, Shalt thou indeed reign over us? or shalt thou indeed have dominion over us? And they hated him yet the more for his dreams, and for his words. And he dreamed yet another dream, and told it to his brethren, and said, Behold, I have dreamed a dream more; and, behold, the sun and the moon and the eleven stars made obeisance to me. And he told it to his father, and to his brethren: and his father rebuked him, and said unto him, What is this dream that thou hast dreamed? Shalt I and thy mother and thy brethren indeed come to bow down ourselves to thee to the earth? (Gen. 37:7-10)

Are you reminded that Jesus made claims of favoritism and divine sonship that brought forth outrageous hatred from the Jews?

> He trusted in God; let him deliver him now, if he will have him: for he said, I am the Son of God. (Matt. 27:43)

Indeed, Jesus himself claimed to be the Son of God. Christ's unique divinity is not just a claim of man. And he, like Joseph, was hated for this claim and for rejecting the ways of the world.

> The world cannot hate you; but me it hateth, because I testify of it, that the works thereof are evil. (John 7:7)

One day Joseph went to find his brothers.

> And when they saw him afar off, even before he came near unto them, they conspired against him to slay him. (Gen. 37:18)

> And they took him, and cast him into a pit: and the pit was empty, there was no water in it. (Gen. 37:24)

Here we see a perfect parallel. With Joseph playing the role of Jesus, and his brothers the Jews of Jesus' day, the conspiracy results in Jesus descending to the lower parts of the earth, Joseph's pit that contained no water. The subsequent lifting of Joseph from the pit to a position of high authority in Egypt is a picture-prophecy of Jesus rising from the grave to be seated at the right hand of God.

> And Pharaoh said unto Joseph, See, I have set thee over all the land of Egypt. And Pharaoh took off his ring from his hand, and put it upon Joseph's hand, and arrayed him in vestures of fine linen, and put a

gold chain about his neck; And he made him to ride in the second chariot which he had; and they cried before him, Bow the knee: and he made him ruler over all the land of Egypt. (Gen. 41:41-43)

Genesis is a long book, recording several thousand years of mankind's history. God inspired the author of Genesis to record these particular stories not only to reveal the history of man and the birth of the nation Israel but to acquaint Israel with Jesus.

When Jesus came several thousand years later, the Jewish people, quite familiar with the stories of Genesis, had already been introduced to the virgin birth, the sacrificial blood to be spilled on the cross, the protection and safety gained from accepting the coat of skin (signifying their acceptance of the blood sacrifice) and entering into Christian fellowship (ark), the hill of sacrifice (Mt. Moriah), the three days in the grave, and the raising up from the grave and exaltation above the earth. Isn't it thrilling to see Christ so vividly portrayed in the Old Testament? Why He has not been accepted by the Jews and the world as a whole today is beyond me.

The study of Jesus in the Old Testament (and remember, we have only viewed six accounts in Genesis), and the study of prophecy and its fulfillment, are two of the most convincing mountains of evidence of the reality of an Almighty God able to see the past and future in a single glance; a God who loves us enough to provide all the solutions we need to live a rich, abundant life and a rewarding afterlife; a God who asks nothing in return except that we believe in His Son, offer worship and praise to Him, and help others to understand how to dissolve barriers in their own lives. So little required for so much given—don't you agree?

13

*The most significant evidence for the deity of Jesus
unfurls in the luminous study of biblical typology.
That Moses was a type, a symbol, an allusion to
Jesus, is profoundly evident when we study . . .*

The Mystery of Jesus in Moses

All the events surrounding the birth and life of Moses
are for one purpose: God is telling the world about Jesus.
It is more than coincidence that throughout the Old
Testament the life and meaning of Jesus is so clearly
revealed. God intended it. Jesus himself said, "Search the
scriptures [the Old Testament]; for in them ye think ye
have eternal life: and they are they which testify of me"
(John 5:39).

Let's take one very small section in the Old Testament
and see if Jesus is in it. Moses, the deliverer of the children of Israel, is a symbol of Jesus, the deliverer of Christians. Moses himself alluded to the typology in Deut.
18:15 (see John 1:21; 7:40). Let's look at the second chapter
of Exodus, which tells of the early years of Moses, and
see if it reveals anything more about Jesus.

And there went a man of the house of Levi, and took
to wife a daughter of Levi. And the woman conceived, and bare a son: and when she saw him that he
was a goodly child, she hid him three months. (Exod.
2:1-2)

If you were to walk up to a stranger on the street
and ask, "Who comes to mind when I say, 'A woman

conceived and bare a son'?" you would most likely hear, "Mary and Jesus." In the opening verses of Exodus 2, as God begins to tell the story of Moses, we are immediately drawn to a picture of the virgin and her child. The selection of these words was inspired by God. He wants all Scriptures to remind us of Jesus. It was Moses himself who actually penned Exodus. The birth of Moses occurred 1500 years before the birth of Jesus. But today as we read over these ancient Scriptures, at the first mention of the infant Moses, our thoughts are directed to the infant Jesus. It is as though God were saying, "Here is a parallel story of My Son. Study the events well, so when I send him, you will know him."

Even the opening sentence of this biography, the bringing together of the parents, is an allusion to the opening sentence in the biography of Jesus.

Now the birth of Jesus Christ was on this wise: When as his mother Mary was espoused to Joseph, before they came together, she was found with child of the Holy Ghost. (Matt. 1:18)

Verse two says Moses was a "goodly" child. Dr. Luke, writing in Acts 7:22, adds that Moses was learned, wise, and mighty in words and deeds. Again we are reminded of the perfection of Jesus and the words used to describe Him in His youth, "And Jesus increased in wisdom and stature, and in favour with God and man" (Luke 2:52).

At the close of verse two, we see that Moses is hidden for three months by his parents. Why? Verse 22 tells us the king of the land charged, "Every son that is born ye shall cast him into the river, and every daughter ye shall save alive." Isn't this the same charge we find the king of Palestine making at the birth of Jesus, to kill all male children up to two years of age?

> Then Herod, when he saw that he was mocked of the wise men, was exceeding wroth, and sent forth, and slew all the children that were in Bethlehem, and in all the coasts thereof, from two years old and under. (Matt. 2:16)

Matthew goes on to say that Jesus' parents are informed of Herod's intentions and they hide Him, just as Moses was hidden (Matt. 2:13). Where? In Egypt, the same country in which Moses was hidden. For how long? Assuming Jesus was born in December, and that His parents departed for Egypt shortly thereafter, and assuming King Herod died in March, which is stated by the first-century historian Josephus, Jesus would have remained hidden three months—the same as Moses. Can all these parallel events be purely coincidental, or was God telling the early Hebrews about Jesus long before He was born, so they would recognize the Deliverer when he came?

Let us continue in this biography of Moses (or is it really a biography of Jesus?).

> And when she could not longer hide him, she took for him an ark of bulrushes, and daubed it with slime and with pitch, and put the child therein; and she laid it in the flags by the river's brink. And his sister stood afar off, to wit what would be done to him. (Exod. 2:3-4)

After the three months' hiding, the infant Moses was placed in an ark and floated on the Nile River near the papyrus rushes. This is a picture of the salvation of Israel. If the basket had sunk, Israel would have remained in bondage, because their deliverer would have died. The basket as a symbol has the same meaning as Noah's ark, which lifted eight godly people (the potential human race) above death, and as the ark of the covenant, the container that carried the law of Moses (Ten Commandments) out of the wilderness. All three of these arks represented Jesus, the ark of salvation, the only one who can lift us out of this world and into a new world. Each of the Old Testament arks represents life to a race of people. Jesus said, "I am the life" (John 14:6). He is the true Ark, represented by Moses floating safely above the deadly waters.

Also notice that Moses' kin "stood afar off" to witness what would happen. Would Moses die or would he live to deliver Israel? Doesn't this remind you of Jesus' kin, His mother and the others at the crucifixion "looking on afar off" (Mark 15:40) to witness what would happen? Would Jesus die or would He live to deliver mankind?

Moses' biography continues:

And the daughter of Pharaoh came down to wash herself at the river; and her maidens walked along by the river's side; and when she saw the ark among the flags, she sent her maid to fetch it. (Exod. 2:5)

It is here at the water's edge that Moses is given over to the world of the Egyptians. His ark is found by Pharaoh's daughter, who had come to the river to cleanse herself. Can we call it coincidental that when Jesus left the safety of His home in Nazareth and entered into His ministry in a sin-filled world, His entrance occurred also at a river's edge, a river where people had come to cleanse themselves?

Then cometh Jesus from Galilee to Jordan unto John, to be baptized of him. (Matt. 3:13)

As Pharaoh's daughter opened the basket, the baby Moses caught sight of the new world he was about to enter, the world of slavery, persecution, sin, and idol worshiping. In Exodus is recorded Moses' response, simple and direct, "the babe wept."

And when she had opened it, she saw the child: and, behold, the babe wept. And she had compassion on him, and said, This is one of the Hebrews' children. (Exod. 2:6)

Fifteen hundred years later Jesus stood upon the Mount of Olives and looked over Jerusalem, the world of evil, sin, and worshipers of man-made laws. His response as He was about to enter is recorded likewise, "He wept over it" (Luke 19:41).

Exodus reveals more similarities between Jesus and Moses.

Then said his sister to Pharaoh's daughter, Shall I go and call to thee a nurse of the Hebrew women, that she may nurse the child for thee? And Pharaoh's daughter said unto her, Go. And the maid went and called the child's mother. And Pharaoh's daughter said unto her, Take this child away, and nurse it for me, and I will give thee thy wages. And the woman took the child, and nursed it. (Exod. 2:7-9)

Miriam, Moses' sister, came forth from the river bank and offered to fetch a Hebrew woman to nurse the babe. She retrieved Moses' very own mother, who took the child, nursed him for several years, received her wages, and returned him to Pharaoh's daughter. Moses was property of the worldly Egyptians but was allowed to be reared by his parents.

Jesus too was property of the world and wages were paid for Him (Luke 2:22-24; Num. 18:15) but like Moses, He was allowed to be reared by His own parents (Luke 2:51). It is also noteworthy that Miriam is the Hebrew rendering of the name Mary. Each detail of the events in the life of Moses reminds us of Jesus. The whole event was a foreshadowing to the Hebrew people that someday this story would repeat itself and would be a sign that the real Deliverer had come.

The story of Moses continues:

> And the child grew, and she brought him unto Pharaoh's daughter, and he became her son. And she called his name Moses: and she said, Because I drew him out of the water. (Exod. 2:10)

When Pharaoh's daughter received the young child she named him Moses, which means to "draw out" of the water. Moses officially entered the world of the Egyptians, the world of sin and persecution, when he was drawn out of the water.

Jesus also officially entered the sinful world to which He was to minister, when He was drawn out of the Jordan River at His baptism.

> And Jesus, when he was baptized, went up straightway out of the water. (Matt. 3:16)

Hebrew lads became men at age thirteen and carried full responsibilities of an adult by their late teens. Yet Moses and Jesus were held back and allowed to mature in wisdom before beginning their ministries; Jesus was thirty

(Luke 3:23) and Moses eighty (Acts 7:23, 29-30).

And it came to pass in those days, when Moses was grown, that he went out unto his brethren, and looked on their burdens: and he spied an Egyptian smiting an Hebrew, one of his brethren.

Frequently the Gospels record how Jesus "looked upon" the people (Mark 3:5, 8:33, 10:21), in much the same manner as Moses "looked on the burdens" of his fellow Hebrews. If we skip over to Exod. 3:10 for a moment, we will see that Moses was chosen by God to deliver His people, the Hebrews, out of Egypt where they were slaves. He was the deliverer. And it was Jesus, the chosen of God who was sent to deliver His people, the Christians, out of the world of sin. Moses' physical leadership and deliverance was an earthly symbol of Jesus' spiritual leadership and deliverance. In both cases, it was the audible voice of God that initiated each ministry, Moses at the burning bush ("God called unto him out of the midst of the bush" [Exod. 3:4]) and Jesus at His baptism ("And lo a voice from heaven, saying, This is my beloved Son, in whom I am well pleased" [Matt. 3:17]).

In verse 12 Moses confronts an oppressor, the enemy of his people. He destroys him and buries him in the firey, hot desert sands for all eternity.

And he looked this way and that way, and when he saw that there was no man, he slew the Egyptian, and hid him in the sand.

This scene is a symbol of an event Jesus is yet to fulfill. But we are assured He will by John the revelator who, in a supernatural vision of the future, sees Jesus destroy the enemy and bury him in the lake of fire for all eternity.

And the devil that deceived them was cast into the lake of fire and brimstone, where the beast and the false prophet are, and shall be tormented day and night for ever and ever. (Rev. 20:10)

As Moses returned to the scene the next day after defeating the enemy, there were two men standing and arguing. Moses' attempt to reconcile the two men is rejected.

And when he went out the second day, behold, two men of the Hebrews strove together: and he said to him that did the wrong, Wherefore smitest thou thy fellow? And he said, Who made thee a prince and a judge over us? intendest thou to kill me, as thou killest the Egyptian? And Moses feared, and said, Surely this thing is known. (Exod. 2:13-14)

Moses' own people, the Hebrews, rejected him. Acts 7:25 adds that Moses "supposed his brethren would have understood how that God by his hand would deliver them: but they understood not." "Where is your authority to judge?" they asked.

Jesus met this same statement from the Jews of His day who asked for a "sign of his authority" (Matt. 12:38). In Luke 19:41-44 is recorded the total rejection of Jesus by the Hebrew race on Palm Sunday. Rejected, just like Moses, by His own people.

The biography of Moses continues.

Now when Pharaoh heard this thing, he sought to slay Moses. But Moses fled from the face of Pharaoh, and dwelt in the land of Midian: and he sat down by a well.

Again in the biography of Moses we are reminded of an account in the life of Jesus, recorded in John 4. John the Baptist had just been sent to prison and, since Jesus was collecting a greater following than John, He feared His ministry and life would be in danger. Jesus broke camp in northern Judea and fled north through Samaria. There He came upon a well, sat down, and talked to a woman— just like Moses. Furthermore, we can hardly overlook the similarity between the names of the two foes (Pharaoh and Pharisees).

Now the priest of Midian had seven daughters: and they came and drew water, and filled the troughs to water their father's flock. And the shepherds came and drove them away: but Moses stood up and helped them, and watered their flock. And when they came to Reuel their father, he said, How is it that ye are come so soon to day? And they said, An Egyptian delivered us out of the hand of the shepherds, and also drew water enough for us, and watered the flock.

At the well, the daughters of Midian's priest were prevented from drawing water by shepherds who chased the girls' flock away. Moses arrived and helped the girls. By now we can see the priest is symbolic of God, the daughters are God's children, Moses is Jesus, and the shepherds are the children of Satan in the world who keep us from the water hole. Jesus will stand up for us and chase the evil shepherds away. He will provide our drink. Jesus told the Samaritan woman at Jacob's well, "Whosoever drinketh of the water that I shall give him shall never thirst" (John 4:14).

Notice in Exodus that the girls said Moses *delivered* them and *quenched their thirst.* Doesn't Jesus do the same; He delivers us from sin into eternal life, and He provides for our daily needs. The person who waits for old age to accept Christ has missed half the reward, missed in fact, life on earth.

Exodus continues:

> And he said unto his daughters, And where is he? why is it that ye have left the man? call him, that he may eat bread.

Here now is revealed a sad truth. After Moses delivered the girls and gave them water, they forgot him, left him stranded. But their father, the priest, reminded them to invite him for fellowship. Haven't many of us forgotten the One who delivered us? God is constantly reminding us to invite Jesus into our lives for fellowship. How do *you* answer this question put to the daughters of the priest: "Where is he? why is it that ye have left the man?"

> And Moses was content to dwell with the man: and he gave Moses Zipporah his daughter. And she bare him a son, and he called his name Gershom: for he said, I have been a stranger in a strange land. And it came to pass in process of time, that the king of Egypt died: and the children of Israel sighed by reason of the bondage, and they cried, and their cry came up unto God by reason of the bondage. And God heard their groaning, and God remembered his covenant with Abraham, with Isaac, and with Jacob. And God looked upon the children of Israel, and God had respect unto them.

Because there was contentment in Moses' fellowship, the priest gave his daughter to be the bride of Moses. The marriage of Jesus to God's children, the church, has not yet occurred, but the Bible says it will. This great wedding is called the marriage supper of the Lamb (see Rev. 19:7-9). Jesus will be wed to the church, the children of God, during the last days of the Great Tribulation period on earth. This wedding will be held in heaven.

Moses was a stranger in any land. In Egypt where he spent the first forty years of his life, he was rejected by both the Hebrews and the Egyptians; in Midian where he spent the next forty years he was a stranger. There he met God in the burning bush and returned to Egypt to lead the mass exodus of the Hebrew race out of slavery. Then he spent forty years a stranger with the rebellious Israelites passing through the Sinai wilderness. Moses died on the mountain just before Joshua led the children of Israel into the Promised Land. His life story is told between Exodus 2 and Deuteronomy 34.

Jesus too was a stranger in all lands. He was rejected in His home town of Nazareth (Matt. 13:54-58), by the Jews of Galilee (John 6:66), by the half-breed race of Samaria (Luke 9:53), by the Pharisees of Judea (John 5:18), by the Greeks on the east side of the Sea of Galilee (Luke 8:37), and most unfortunately by a great number of people today.

The good news in the Bible is that God has sent a Deliverer to set people free and to feed them daily. He is a spiritual Deliverer, and to help people identify Him when He came, God raised up Moses, the physical deliverer whose birth and circumstances of life so clearly foreshadow those of Jesus. Isn't it obvious? Over fifty circumstances and events found in just *one* chapter of *one* Old Testament book remind us of Jesus and His ministry. Do Jesus a favor. Read this chapter, "The Mystery of Jesus in Moses," to one of Moses' descendants, one of your Jewish friends. He has somehow overlooked a lot of what God has to show and tell.

14

For centuries man has sought to escape death. Yet there is only one power in the universe strong enough to defeat death—the power of God. In His message to man, God explains the key to releasing this power.

The Secret to Everlasting Life

In the spring of 1491 B.C. (there is some debate concerning the exact date) God decided to set His people, the Hebrews, free. They had been in Egyptian bondage 400 years. God called forth a leader, Moses, and bestowed ten great plagues upon Pharaoh and the Egyptians (Exodus, chapters 2-11). When the night of the Exodus came, God gave Moses specific instructions on what he and the Israelites must do before they could leave Egypt. The instructions were peculiar, but if the Israelites would obey, they would be free. Obedience was the key. Here, paraphrased, is what God said in Exodus 12.

From your flocks, each family must take a young, unblemished lamb and kill it. The leg must not be broken. It must be slaughtered so the blood will spill. With a hyssop branch, smear some blood above and on both sides of the doorpost outside your home. Then roast the lamb on an open fire, and eat it all with unleavened bread and bitter herbs. Eat fully dressed, in haste, with staff in hand.

In the night I will pass through Egypt and kill the firstborn of every family which has not applied the blood [mainly, the Egyptians]. I will pass over [thus the term, Passover] the homes where I see the blood and none will die. If you obey me, I will deliver you from bondage.

That night two to three million Israelites obeyed and were freed from Pharaoh and the taskmasters. God opened the passage of the Red Sea for the great Exodus, then closed the sea behind them, shutting out the enemy.

God's message of obedience is repeated throughout the Bible. It is stated often, and many times it is implied or suggested as God's people act out a command to display their faith. Obedience to God is the key to releasing the power of heaven, as we see in the Passover event. So powerful is this heavenly power that not only did it set the Israelites free from bondage, but it freed them from death. The firstborn of the Egyptians who died that night were not just children. Most were adults, fathers and grandfathers, for many of them too were firstborns.

Why God Instituted the Passover

Why did God give such mysterious instructions? Why didn't He just put the Egyptians to sleep and let the Israelites walk out? First of all He wanted it to be so unusual they would record and remember every detail. He had a reason for this.

By recording and preserving as sacred the Passover events and by repeating the celebration every year, each detail of the Passover became so familiar to the Israelites that soon they would see the underlying truth that God had woven into these events, the *real* reason God chose this peculiar ritual to grant freedom and life to His people.

Secondly He wanted to see if they had enough faith in

His Word to obey every detail. Remember, God did not speak audibly to each family. He simply impressed upon Moses what was to be done, and Moses told three million people of this weird procedure. Would you have obeyed?

God told them to eat fully dressed, because they must be prepared to leave at a moment's notice. They were not to put leaven (yeast) in the bread, because they would not be around long enough for the bread to rise; God planned to deliver them *that night*. The bitter herbs were to remind them of the bitterness of Egypt. The blood on the doorposts was the sign of obedience. God told the Israelites they were to repeat the Passover feast at the same time every year, forever, to remember. By killing the firstborn of every Egyptian family, He was destroying every family tree, every dynasty. Egypt would have to start all over again as a defeated, embarrassed nation.

God used Old Testament people and events to teach us a greater New Testament truth. By studying what God told Moses to do to deliver the Israelites out of the hands of Pharaoh and Egypt and into the Promised Land, we can learn what He expects us to do to be delivered out of the hands of Satan and the world of sin and into eternal life.

Passover Was an Example

Just as the evil Pharaoh ruled Egypt, Satan rules the world of sin. Each of us is born into this fallen world. None is born in the Promised Land (Rom. 3:9). Just as Moses led the Israelites out of slavery, God leads us from the bondage of sin and self. Just as Moses stretched forth his hand to part the Red Sea and allow passage for the escaping Israelites, then closed the sea behind them, God opens the door to heaven and Christian fellowship. If we obey and enter through the door, He will slam it shut behind us, blocking out Satan and the world of sin. Just as the Promised Land of the Israelites is the land of milk and honey, the Christian destination is heaven.

Herein lies the secret to everlasting life, the real truth God was revealing to the world with the peculiar Passover event. To understand and know this truth, we have but to read and study God's Word and make obvious substitutions (see chart on the following page).

For 1500 years the Israelites celebrated the Passover feast in remembrance of their deliverance. They even started a new calendar beginning with the date of Exodus. Each spring they sacrificed the lamb, still not sure why, and ate it with unleavened bread and bitter herbs. Then the fulfillment of the Passover was unveiled.

Jesus—the Real Passover Lamb

The first hint came when John the Baptist introduced Jesus to the world. He didn't say, "This is Jesus of Nazareth" or, "Here is the promised Messiah" or, "Here is our King." He said, "Behold the Lamb of God" (John 1:29). Sheep and goats of Judea had many uses, but the lamb's use was for sacrifice. John was telling the world that God had sent His unblemished, perfect Lamb to be placed upon the sacrificial altar. Jesus was the Lamb.

Three years later it happened. On the exact same afternoon and at the exact same hour that the sacrifice was made in Egypt 1500 years before, Jesus' blood was spilled. The wounds in His hands and around His head from the nails and crown of thorns stained the cross exactly where God had told the Israelites to stain the doorposts outside the home. And there was more blood. His back

Event	Meaning
Pharaoh, the evil leader of opposing physical forces.	*Satan,* the evil leader of opposing spiritual forces.
Egypt, the land where God's people were held in bondage.	*The world,* the fleshly land wherein many are bound and conformed (Rom. 12:2).
Moses, the leader in charge of the Exodus out of bondage.	*God,* the one who sets people free from the bondage of the world.
The Israelites, God's chosen people (Rom. 11:1).	*Christians,* God's chosen people (1 Pet. 2:9).
Slavery, the Israelite's bondage.	*Elements of the world,* the bondage that holds people today (Gal. 4:3).
The Red Sea, the passageway out of Egypt.	The Christian conversion, typified by water baptism, the passage out of earthly bondage.
The Promised Land, the "land of milk and honey" destination of God's people.	*Heaven,* the wonderful destination of Christians.
The lamb, the unblemished sacrifice.	*Jesus,* the sinless sacrifice (1 Pet. 2:21-25).
The blood-stained doorposts, the sign of life to the Israelite families.	*The blood-stained cross,* the sign of life to all who believe (John 6:54).
The leaven, a sign of disobedience, for God said not to use it in the bread.	*Sin,* for God says to keep sin out of our bodies (Rom. 6:12).
The death angel, who represents death to the Egyptian (unbelievers) families.	*Eternal damnation,* the death that awaits all unbelievers (Mark 16:16).
The hyssop branch, a common weed available to all, used to apply the blood.	*Faith,* available to all and is the application of the Christian life.
The bitter herbs, to remember the bitterness of bondage.	*The bitterness in life,* that degree of sorrow all humans experience as we walk through the valley of the shadow of death.
God opening and closing the Red Sea to allow the Israelites through and keep the Egyptians out.	*God opening the door of salvation and fellowship,* and shutting out sin in the lives of Christians (Rev. 3:20).
Eating fully dressed with staff in hand, to show readiness to move quickly, at God's command, to flee Egypt.	*The readiness of Christians* in watching for the second coming of Jesus, and to be prepared to move quickly at his every command (Matt. 24:42).

had up to 468 torn gashes from the possible twelve-thonged scourge, with which he was flogged thirty-nine times (Matt. 27:26). Isaiah said it is these blood-spilling stripes that heal us (Isa. 53:5). And great quantities of blood poured forth from Jesus' heart as He hung on the cross with a soldier's spear hanging from the rib cage of His naked and torn body (John 19:34). The soldiers had come to break His leg to hasten His death (John 19:33) but when they arrived, He was already dead (also see the prophecy in Ps. 34:20). The Lamb's leg was not broken. Jesus tasted the cup of bitterness in Gethsemane and He passed through the fire of death. Some use the roasted lamb as typological proof that Jesus descended into hell during the period His body was in the grave (1 Pet. 3:19).

The Israelites had to apply the blood with hyssop, a common weed readily available. It showed their faith and obedience. We apply the blood of the Lamb in much the same way—by showing our faith (available to all) and obeying the Word of God as found in the Bible. It was the "power in the blood" that saved every Israelite family from a death that night in Egypt. When we show that we accept the cross of Jesus, the spilled blood, the atoning death, and believe that Jesus rose to life after passing through the fire of death, we are applying the blood over our doorpost. Just as the death angel passed over and granted physical life to those who applied the blood, so we will be passed over and granted spiritual life—salvation—first for the soul and then for the body. We can pass into heaven as surely as the Israelites passed into the Promised Land. The greatest event of the Old Testament was the physical Passover and deliverance of the Israelites. The greatest event of the New Testament is the spiritual Passover and deliverance of Christians.

Jesus is the Passover (1 Cor. 5:7).

Passover Versus Easter

Passover and Easter are the same event. It is God giving freedom from death and the world of sin to all who show their faith in accepting the slain Lamb. When Jesus ate His Last Supper (a Passover feast) He extracted two elements, the bread and wine, and instituted Holy Communion. The Passover remembers deliverance from Egypt; Holy Communion remembers God's Lamb and the deliverance from death and sin He has granted.

Have you had your Exodus yet? Your Passover? Have you come out of Egypt and let God close the sea behind you? Have you applied the blood of the slain Lamb to your life? Have you accepted the power of the cross, the power to defeat death and to grant eternal life? The order of events God gave Moses for deliverance is the same order we must follow. Here they are:

Select an *unblemished lamb.* Select the *sinless Jesus,* the Lamb of God.

Sacrifice the lamb. *Accept* Jesus' atoning crucifixion.

Apply the blood. Show your *faith* in obedience.

Roast the lamb. *Believe* that Jesus passed through death before ascending.

Eat the lamb. After salvation *receive nourishment:* study, fellowship, worship, and serve.

Remove the leaven. Get disobedience and *sin out* of your life.

Eat with *staff in hand.* Always *be ready* for the Lord.

Cross the Red Sea. Once in the world of Christianity, let God close the door on the world of *sin behind you.*

PART FOUR

THE SPIRIT WORLD

15

*What is the basis for the gods of ancient mythology?
How do we explain mysterious events? Are there
really invisible creatures sharing this world with us?*

Angels and Other Spirit Creatures

The Bible speaks of several types of spirit beings who
inhabit the earth, space, and a world under the earth.

That at the name of Jesus every knee should bow, of
things in heaven, and things in earth, and things
under the earth. (Phil. 2:10)

And every creature which is in heaven, and on the
earth, and under the earth . . . (Rev. 5:13)

Spirit Creatures of Mythology
Every race of man has written of spirit creatures.
Ancient Babylonians had minor gods who carried messages
to men on earth. Moslem legend has the supernatural
jinn who influenced human affairs. The Romans called
their guardian spirit a *genius* and their half-goat/half-
man deities of the countryside *fauns*. The Greeks spoke
of a similar creature they called a *satyr*. The Greek poet
Hesiod, in the days of Isaiah, wrote, "millions of spiritual
creatures walk the earth." The basis of all these spirit
beings is found in the Bible.

The Bible never denies that spirit creatures exist. In
fact, the Bible mentions spirits over 500 times and even
describes many of them.

Seraphim and Cherubim
In Isa. 6:1-7 we read of *seraphim,* a high-ranking form

of angel that have six wings each and fly about performing certain divine chores.

A similar but less ranking angelic creature, the *cherubim*, is mentioned more frequently. Cherubims were placed east of Eden to guard the entrance to the tree of life when Adam and Eve were driven out (Gen. 3:24). Cherubims are described in Ezekiel (chapters one and ten) as having the likeness of a man, but with four faces resembling man, lion, ox, and eagle. Unlike the seraphim, each cherubim has only *four* wings, and under the wings hands like a man's. Their bodies glow as do burning coals, and they move very swiftly, resembling lightning. When the cherubims move, their wings make a rushing noise, suggesting some form of atmosphere in their heavenly dwelling place.

Spirit Animals and Beasts

Other angelic beings are described in Revelation chapter four and are called *beasts* (KJV) or *creatures* (RSV). There are four of them, each with a different face, each with six wings, and each has a body filled with eyes that see in every direction. Their function is to encircle the throne of God, "and they rest not day and night, saying, Holy, holy, holy, Lord God Almighty, which was, and is, and is to come" (Rev. 4:8).

Besides these angelic-type creatures, the spirit world also contains spirit animals, resembling animals on earth. (See the chapter "Is Heaven a Real Place?")

Archangels

We are told in Col. 1:16 of various ranks and orders in the spirit world. One such rank is a superior form of angel called a chief angel or *archangel*. Dan. 10:13 says there are several such creatures in the kingdom of God, but only one is actually named.

Yet Michael the archangel, when contending with the devil . . . (Jude 9)

Besides Michael, Gabriel is considered to be an archangel, although the Bible never actually states his rank. Gabriel spoke to the prophet Daniel in the sixth century B.C. (Dan. 9:21), and was given the honor of announcing not only the coming birth of John the Baptist to John's father (Luke 1:19), but the virgin conception of our Lord to his mother Mary (Luke 1:26-27). Surely such an honor would have been given to one greater than the rank of common angel.

Lucifer, the fallen angel mentioned in Isaiah 14 and in other verses, was also most likely an archangel, perhaps the most "perfect in beauty" (Ezek. 28:12). In Ezek. 28:14 he is called "the anointed cherub," suggesting the relationship between cherubims and archangels.

The only other angel called by name in the Bible is also a fallen angel, a king of demons named Apollyon, the "angel of the bottomless pit" (Rev. 9:11).

Fallen Angels or Demons

The devils (KJV) or demons (RSV) are mentioned only four times in the Old Testament, but fifty-one times in the New Testament. These creatures are actually angels, spirit beings created by God, who have fallen from grace and joined the ranks of the Ruler of Darkness, Satan. These beings are responsible for the supernatural possessions and occurrences associated with witchcraft and demon worship.

Common Angels

By far the most common of all the spirit beings are the ordinary angels. The Bible says of their number that there are a "thousand thousands . . . and ten thousand times ten thousand" (Dan. 7:10). There are an "innumerable company of angels" (Heb. 12:22).

Angels are an entirely different creature than humans. Humans never become angels. Humans were called into existence by a creative act of God, and they reproduce and die. Angels do neither. Angels were all created at once, in the beginning, long before the planet earth was formed. In speaking to Job, God mentions that when He first formed the earth, all the angels ("sons of God") shouted for joy. They were with Him then.

> Where wast thou when I laid the foundations of the earth . . . when all the sons of God shouted for joy? (Job 38:1-7)

To determine just what an angel looks like and the nature of his character, we must again turn to the Bible.

Here we see that angels have the appearance of ordinary men. They have normal-appearing eyes, hands, head, feet, bodies, and they possess similar attributes: emotions, appetites, pride, anger, lust, and desires; they have limited wisdom, patience, will power, and modesty; they cook and wear garments.

Yet there are differences, too. The Bible says they are superior to men (Ps. 8:5). While the bodies of men are made of the minerals of the earth, those of angels are spiritual bodies. These bodies are very real and of a material substance, but their exact nature is unrevealed. Angels may appear as ordinary men or they may make themselves invisible to humans. Common angels do not possess halos and ordinarily do not have wings. They could appear to us on the street and we would be unaware of their identity.

Be not forgetful to entertain strangers: for thereby some have entertained angels unawares. (Heb. 13:2)

It was common practice in the Bible days to feed and entertain strangers, for there is record of angels visiting as ordinary men. Angels appeared to Abraham and to Lot in Sodom; they appeared to Moses, Joshua, Gideon, Elijah, Daniel, Zacharias, Mary, Jesus, Peter, and John. Over thirty cases are recorded of angels appearing to humans.

While angels may eat food (Ps. 78:25; Gen. 18:2, 8) and mate with humans (Gen. 6:1-2), neither is necessary, and the latter is outside of God's will. These divine creatures are powerful and have mighty bodies. They do not require rest. They can travel faster than the speed of light and frequently ascend and descend between heaven and earth. The apostle Nathanael was given the ability to witness this by Jesus.

And he said unto him, Verily, verily, I say unto you, Hereafter ye shall see heaven open, and the angels of God ascending and descending upon the Son of man. (John 1:51)

Men of the Bible who recognized angels usually trembled and fell to their knees before the extraterrestrial creatures. Often the angel's first words were, "Fear not" (Luke 1:13, 30; 2:10). We are not to fear angels, for they are here to watch over us. Neither are we to worship them, for worship is for God alone (Col. 2:18).

That brings us to the important question as to the function of angels: what are they here for?

What Angels Do for a Living

Job 1:7 tells us that Satan walks the earth to and fro. The angels are messengers of God, and their work is to carry out the redemptive chores of God. God is calling men back into his fold, while Satan is tearing them loose. It is the ministry of the Holy Spirit to oppose Satan in spiritual matters and concerns of Christian growth. The angels minister in a more temporal sense; they aid and watch over Christians in a physical or material way. Not only do they ascend and descend to heaven and earth, but according to Zech. 1:8-10, they also walk to and fro through the earth.

In various Scriptures we see angels in their work: they minister to Christians, guard gates, conduct combat in times of war, give strength in time of trial, direct pastors, witness confessions, attract sinners to witnesses, and deliver answers to prayer. 1 Cor. 11:10 indicates angels are the unseen witnesses of Christians in worship. The work of angels is primarily directed to the Christian.

Are they not all ministering spirits, sent forth to minister for them who shall be heirs of salvation? (Heb. 1:14)

But since this work is redemptive in nature, we find the angels' greatest and busiest times coincide with the first and second coming of our redeemer Jesus Christ.

In the Gospels we see angels ministering often, first to John the Baptist's father, then to Mary. After the birth of Jesus He was "seen of angels" in every period of his life (1 Tim. 3:16). Psalm 91 is prophetically directed to Jesus.

For he shall give his angels charge over thee, to keep thee in all thy ways. (Ps. 91:11)

At the outset of Jesus' ministry, after He had fasted forty days and confronted Satan in the wilderness, "behold, angels came and ministered unto him" (Matt. 4:11). Exactly how they ministered is not known, perhaps to help Him locate food after His fast, perhaps to keep away the wild beasts, perhaps to deliver a message from

God as to His next move.

Throughout Jesus' life there must have been numerous angels hovering invisibly about Him. In Gethsemane, Luke 22:43 says, "And there appeared an angel unto him from heaven, strengthening him." Even after the crucifixion we find angels rolling the stone aside to reveal an empty tomb to a surprised world and later seated in the sepulchre. Even after Jesus ascended, two men, angels, asked why the crowd was staring into the heavens, for this same Jesus who ascended, in like manner will descend.

Just as the first advent of Jesus is a time of great angelic activity, so shall be the second advent, as described by John in the book of Revelation.

The principle dwelling place of angels is in heaven, but they are in the earth also—everywhere where there is a believer. What has been ascribed to providence is the work of angels: in time of sorrow, in times of great need; a runaway car is miraculously turned aside; a baby swallows a pin and it passes through the digestive tract without harm; we are miraculously delivered from death or accident—all the while the angels are with us ministering, protecting, watching, listening—helping our prayers to be answered—creating a hedge about us.

Are Angels Seen Today?

There *are* those today who have actually seen these wonderful messengers of God. We do not know why certain individuals are allowed to see the angels, any more than we know why certain individuals are miraculously healed while others, just as strong in faith, are not. One such man whom I know personally and respect admirably for his love of God and consent to serve is Dr. Charles M. Leaming, pastor, radio minister, and founder of Florida Beacon College. In his book *I Saw Angels* Dr. Leaming gives the following testimony (used by permission):

It was in the summer of 1939. I was the camp-meeting speaker at Mirror Lake, between Seattle and Tacoma, Washington. We were in the midst of a great revival meeting there. I was scheduled to be back in Ottumwa, Iowa, at Hickory Grove, where the year before, in the spring of 1938, Clint Baker, the owner and operator of a large nightclub and dance hall on Highway 63, about four miles southeast of Ottumwa, was wonderfully saved. He gave the entire property to us for a revival meeting. It later became a famous campground, known as Hickory Grove Campground, which is still in operation, and thousands of souls have been saved, filled with the Spirit, and many called to preach the Gospel of Jesus Christ there at Hickory Grove.

When I arrived at Hickory Grove in the midst of the meeting, there was a real binding spirit. It seemed that all hell was turned loose. When the invitation was given and they came around the altar to pray, it just seemed that you couldn't pray. I continued to pray with the people around the altar for some time, and after a while I stepped outside. I heard voices coming from the distance, probably a city block from the tent. I said to a fellow pastor, "I'm going down to see what's going on. I'll be back in a few minutes."

I walked down to the place which we have since called "Inspiration Point" because of this experience. I noticed a cluster of people standing on the point. In fact, there were eleven altogether. Among this group of eleven, there was a young man by the name of Charles Piper, who is now pastor of the Open Bible Tabernacle in St. Petersburg, Florida. Leonard and Dolora Collett, who are now pastors of the First Church of the Open Bible in

Ottumwa, Iowa, were also there. All three of these young people were called of God to preach the Gospel, and they went out into the ministry from the church there in Ottumwa.

As I approached the group, Charles Piper stepped up to me, with tears streaming down his cheeks, and said to me, "Brother Leaming, there are angels over there. Look!" I looked across the creek. There were no trees on the hillside, but it was covered with beautiful green grass. As I looked, I saw two beings clothed in shining white raiment. They were the most graceful beings that I have ever seen in my life. They would walk a few feet apart from each other, and then they would come back together again. What a graceful sight!

A shaft of golden light came out of the north and followed the course of the creek. This shaft of light tapered off as a sword. It followed the course of the creek, and came down to the spot where these beings appeared on the hillside. Suddenly the light went directly out of its course, turned, and played above the heads of these two angelic beings for several minutes.

As we watched this golden shaft of light, which tapered off at the end like a sword, all of us stood there weeping. There was one lady that was stricken under the power of God, lying prostrate upon the ground. We realized that we were witnessing a manifestation of God; actually witnessing the appearance of angels.

Suddenly they were gone. They disappeared. The angels and the shaft of golden light that tapered off as a sword were gone. We stood there for a little while longer, weeping, praising the Lord. Finally, I turned to those around me and said to them, "This is apparently all that God wants to do at this time. Let's go back to the tent." The following paragraph is the personal testimony given by Rev. Charles H. Piper who was also among those witnessing this phenomenal sight.

In the summer of 1939 my wife and I attended the Hickory Grove Camp Meeting five miles south of Ottumwa, Iowa. Following an evening service, about eleven of us went to a hillside called Inspiration Point to pray. While kneeling in prayer I glanced across a little ravine and there on the hillside I saw what I thought was two ladies dressed in white. I had a very powerful flashlight and I walked closer to them and when I turned on the light they disappeared! When I turned the light off they reappeared. I called the others' attention and as we stood there in amazement, Brother Leaming came down the hill and joined us. The two figures left the hillside and came directly across the ravine without going down into the valley and stood within twenty feet of the group. They stayed there for about 30 seconds and then floated back to the hillside. Suddenly there was a flash of light and they disappeared; they did not return to the hillside again. We were all convinced that we had had a rare and wonderful privilege of seeing two of God's heavenly beings. I feel they were angels.

We went back to the tent, and immediately we felt that this spirit of bondage was gone. The glory of God came down on that meeting with such power that it is really impossible to describe how great it was. In fact, it turned out to be an all-night meeting. After we had prayed and waited upon the Lord in the tent for hours, we marched all around the campground, praising and rejoicing in the Lord, until daybreak the next morning.

The Spirit of God was exceedingly present that night. These angels apparently were sent as special help from heaven to minister unto us. As a result that camp meeting turned into one of the greatest soul-winning revivals that I have ever known. It went on and on for weeks.

One night during the meeting, a group of men had a burden to pray for a man whom they had worked with at the John Morrell Packing House in Ottumwa. These men had just recently taken Christ as their Saviour. They were attending the service, but they got up and left the service without telling anyone where they were going. They got into a pickup truck and drove down to the man's house. The man was in bed, and they got him up and witnessed to him of the saving grace of the Lord Jesus Christ. The man surrendered his life to Christ. Before the service was over, the men came back, and as they were coming in, you could hear them singing, "All of my burdens went rolling away, rolling away, down at the Saviour's Cross."

This is just a part of the story of how the meeting turned into a great soul-saving revival.

The same night that these angelic beings appeared, there was an incident involving a truck-driver of the small town of Moravia, Iowa. This truck-driver was unsaved. I didn't hear about his story until after this experience with the angels, but later he told us of the angels appearing to him. This man, who was then unsaved, was driving his truck past the tent. As he was driving by, he saw these angels pass over the road in front of him, down to the hillside where we witnessed them. That was the same night that we witnessed this tremendous scene of the visitation of angels.

The man was so frightened by what he saw, that he stepped on the gas and went home; but before he went to sleep, he knelt and surrendered his life to Jesus Christ.

When he heard us tell of the event when the angels appeared, he told us the story of what happened to him on that identical night.

People can say that they believe we had a dream, but I want you to know that we were not asleep. It wasn't a vision. There were twelve of us that saw this at the same time. There was no question in my mind but that they were actual angels who came to minister to us in that critical time.

Let us refer to Heb. 1:14 again: "Are they not all ministering spirits, sent forth to minister for them, who shall be heirs of salvation?" It is not the purpose of angels to bring salvation to us, but rather they are to minister to us after we have received salvation through faith in the Lord Jesus Christ. They are to minister to us and help us.

Heb. 12:22 and 23: "But ye are come unto Mount Sion, and unto the city of the Living God, the heavenly Jerusalem, and to an innumerable company of angels, To the general assembly and church of the firstborn, which are written in heaven." Those which are born again by the Holy Spirit, and whose names are written in the Lamb's Book of Life.

There is an innumerable company of angels that comes to minister to the Body of Christ, wherever they are met together in the Name of the Lord Jesus Christ. They testify to the fact that Jesus is the Mediator of the New Covenant.

So now we know that angels are real. We know that they are heavenly beings. They are celestial beings. And that even though they are spirits, they can also appear.

16

Citizens of earth are under the influence of a powerful, evil person. He affects all our lives. From the Bible we learn of his creation, his activities since the dreadful day he fell from grace, and his destiny.

Who Is Satan?

Satan, the recipient of blame for the ills of mankind—is he for real or not? Evil, like a disease, has a tangible cause. For thousands of years the world knew of diseases, but only recently have we seen the real germs causing the disease. Just as assuredly we have known evil but have not yet seen the real germ of evil. But he is there just the same.

How do we know Satan is a real person and not just a principle or a force? The evidence is in the Bible.

Satan Is a Person
The Bible treats this producer of evil (whom we call Satan) as a real person. He provoked King David (1 Chron. 21:1); he spoke (Job 1:7); he stood (Ps. 109:6). He is consistently referred to by use of a masculine, personal pronoun. Jesus treated him as a real person (Luke 13:16) and talked with him (Matt. 4:3). The apostles treated him as a person (1 Thess. 2:18), and warned against his intrusion (Eph. 4:27).

In the Bible Satan is given several personal names: Satan (Rev. 12:9), Beelzebub (Matt. 10:25), Belial (2 Cor. 6:15), and Lucifer (Isa. 14:12-14).

Repeatedly the Bible treats Satan as a real being who

influences people to evil. Satan is not the evil any more than the germ is the disease. He draws people into evil, ignorance, and darkness. He is not the sole source of temptation. We are also tempted by the world and its riches, as well as being under the reign of our own body chemistry, sometimes called "the flesh." Knowing that Satan is a real being, we can rightly ask where he came from, why he is here, and what will happen to him.

The Perfect Angel

In Old Testament days God spoke to the arrogant Job and asked, "Where were you when I laid the foundations of the earth. . . . and all the sons of God [angels] shouted for joy?" (Job 38:4, 7, RSV). God is saying that long before Job, before Adam and before earth was created, there were heavens and many angels. This era was the dispensation of angels, heavenly beings created by God with greater intelligence and powers than humans. Our Bible only tells us the story of the earth and its inhabitants, the dispensation of man. But in a few locations God gives us a glimpse of the dispensation of angels. The Job passage is one of these glimpses.

In Ezek. 28:1-11 God gives Ezekiel a message for the proud "prince" or leader of Tyre. However, in 28:12 a message is given for the "king" of Tyre. The description of the king reveals this person to be none other than Satan himself, the evil power behind the prince of Tyre. In this message, God offers a glimpse of His greatest created being, His most perfect creature, the leader of the multitude of angels. Here is how it reads in the Bible.

Moreover the word of the Lord came unto me, saying, Son of man, take up a lamentation upon the king of Tyrus, and say unto him, Thus saith the Lord God; Thou sealest up the sum, full of wisdom, and perfect in beauty. Thou hast been in Eden the garden of God; every precious stone was thy covering . . . the workmanship of thy tabrets and of thy pipes was prepared in thee in the day that thou wast created. Thou art the anointed cherub that covereth; and I have set thee so: thou wast upon the holy mountain of God; thou hast walked up and down in the midst of the stones of fire. Thou wast perfect in thy ways from the day that thou wast created, till iniquity was found in thee. (Ezek. 28:11-15)

We know God is speaking about Satan here, because He says, "Thou hast been in Eden the garden of God." According to the first-century historian Josephus, the literal king of Tyre in Ezekiel's day was an evil man who exalted himself as God. This message from God to Ezekiel is directed to both the literal king and the one who instills the evil nature of this king. Notice that God says he is "full of wisdom and perfect in beauty." Also that he "wast created." Men are not *created*; they are *born* through a reproductive process. Satan "wast perfect"; he was created an angel, an "anointed cherub." Then something happened: "iniquity was found in thee."

The Fall of Satan

In verses 16 through 19 God says because of his sin, this perfect angel will be destroyed: "therefore will I bring forth a fire from the midst of thee, it shall devour thee."

Then God reveals no more of this person. But to Isaiah,

another glimpse is given to help fill the gaps.

Isaiah 14 foresees that Israel's independence will be restored as the king of Babylon becomes powerless and falls. Again, in verse 12, the story shifts to the real power behind the king. God expounds on the king of Babylon's fall, then speaks through the literal king directly to the source of his evil power, to the same angel described in Ezekiel. He is called by name, "Lucifer, son of the morning." This "speaking through" is the same technique used by Jesus when He spoke "through" Peter and addressed Satan who was controlling him (Matt. 16:21-23). A similar example is when He spoke "through" the demon-possessed man and addressed the demon directly (Mark 1:23-26).

> How art thou fallen from heaven, O Lucifer, son of the morning! how art thou cut down to the ground, which didst weaken the nations! For thou hast said in thine heart, I will ascend into heaven, I will exalt my throne above the stars of God: I will sit also upon the mount of the congregation, in the sides of the north: I will ascend above the heights of the clouds; I will be like the most high. Yet thou shalt be brought down to hell, to the sides of the pit. (Isa. 14:12-15)

In this brief passage God reveals the name of this perfect created angel and gives the reasons why he was cut off from the kingdom of God and cast down upon the earth. This all happened eons before man was created. But from John 1:1 and 1:14 we know that Jesus was there, and He witnessed this dramatic event. He says so.

> And he said unto them, I beheld Satan as lightning fall from heaven. (Luke 10:18)

The Fall of Angels

In Matt. 25:41 Jesus speaks of the devil "and his angels." So there must have been many angels cast out with Lucifer. We also read here that hell was "prepared" for Satan and his angels. In 2 Pet. 2:4 we read that God "spared not the angels that sinned, but cast them down to hell, and delivered them into chains of darkness." And in Jude 6 we read, "And the angels which kept not their first estate, but left their own habitation, he hath reserved in everlasting chains under darkness unto the judgment of the great day."

So Lucifer was cast from heaven because of pride, and with him went thousands of "fallen angels." These angels became devils or demons, and Lucifer became Satan, the prince of devils (Matt. 9:34), the prince of the world (John 14:30).

Before you begin to feel sorry for this beautiful but fallen creature, remember he was a murderer and liar from the beginning (John 8:44). God did not create him that way, but did create him with a free will to choose right from wrong. We are all familiar with this freedom; God gave it to us, too. Lucifer chose his ego. By successfully tempting Eve, he brought to our race death, labor in childbirth, and weeds in our crops (which, by the way, cost the world billions of dollars annually—read Gen. 3:14-19).

Satan is also the enemy who sows the weeds of the world that chokes out a fruitful crop of spiritual growth (Matt. 13:39). While Satan has the power of death on the world, Jesus, through His unique death and resurrection, has provided a way to defeat the sting of death (Heb. 2:14).

Satan Influences Mankind

In Adam's day, Satan regained dominion and began to

tempt and influence mankind. We live in his domain. How this fallen angel has induced his evil venom upon mankind is also recorded in the Bible.

In Daniel, chapter 10, for instance, Daniel tells how as he stood by the Tigris River in April, an angel came and visited him. Daniel fainted but was revived. The angel told him his prayers were heard the first day they were given, but for twenty-one days Satan prevented God's messenger from reaching Daniel. Michael the archangel had to come and help the angel break through the satanic wall surrounding Daniel. In this reference we see that Satan has the power (and uses it) to block angels.

In Zech. 3:1 we read of a similar occurrence whereby Zechariah saw Satan standing next to the angel of the Lord, resisting the high priest who desired access to the angel.

In 2 Cor. 4:4 we are told that Satan, the god of this world, blinds the minds of the unbelievers, making it difficult for them to see "the light of the glorious gospel of Christ."

In Eph. 6:11 we read that Satan uses subtle techniques of trickery, called "wiles," to lure his victims into darkness.

In 2 Thess. 2:9 we read that he uses "all power and signs and lying wonders." He especially uses his influence in our weaker moments. He tempted Jesus as He was fasting for forty days in the wilderness above the lower Jordan Valley (Matt. 4:3) and later as Jesus endured His most trying moment in the Garden of Gethsemane just before He was arrested (Mark 14:32-42).

According to the Apostle John in John 13:2, it was Satan who instilled within the heart of Judas Iscariot the notion of betrayal.

Satan has the ability to snare his captives at will (2 Tim. 2:26). He is the deceiver of the whole world (Rev. 12:9). He is even able to influence humans to the point of insanity (Mark 5:1-18), blindness and dumbness (Matt. 12:22), convulsions and suicidal attempts (Luke 9:39).

Resist Satan and He Will Flee

Indeed the evil powers that influence us are great but God has not left us without a defense. In 1 Pet. 5:8-9 we are told to resist Satan who "as a roaring lion, walketh about, seeking whom he may devour."

In Eph. 6:11 we are told to arm ourselves with the full armor of God, to use all the powers of faith and prayer to resist Satan.

And we are assured in James 4:7 that if we resist him he will flee.

Exactly why God permitted Satan to regain a foothold when the deceiver convinced Adam and Eve to commit that first sin remains a mystery. Perhaps this is one of God's secrets mentioned in Deut. 29:29.

For sure God knew this would happen and therefore allowed it to come to pass. We may be close to God's reasoning if we observe that for humans to choose right there must be a wrong, an opposition to right. Could it be that God permits evil forces controlled by Satan to exist so that we will have the privilege to exercise one of the greatest gifts God gave us—free will? Can you teach a child to swim if you never let go of him, or never place him in the deadly waters? God allows us to experience the water, but He has given us an Ark to climb upon— Jesus—and He has instructed us how to swim to that Ark. God knows the world is controlled by Satan but if we are to learn to swim (part of our growing up) He must allow

Satan to exist. God now stands in the Ark shouting directions: swim (John 1:12), swim (Acts 4:12), *swim* (Acts 6:31).

God has given us special glimpses of the story of Satan—his creation, his fall, his regaining dominion over the earth, and the evil he has caused. But the story would not be complete if the destiny of Satan was left untold. God has spared us this enigma and revealed Satan's destiny.

The Defeat of Satan

The first hint appears in Gen. 3:14-15, where we are told that Satan is cursed for all of eternity for bringing sin and death into the world.

In 1 John 3:8 we read a profound statement.

> He that committeth sin is of the devil; for the devil sinneth from the beginning. For this purpose the Son of God was manifested, that he might destroy the works of the devil.

The reason Jesus took on a fleshly form and entered our earthly system, subjecting himself to Satanic temptations and our natural laws, was to do away with the work of Satan, to annul his evil spell and provide an exit for those who choose to believe.

In Col. 2:15 we read that Jesus crashed Satan's party and "spoiled principalities and powers." As He stood in the temple at Jerusalem a few days before He was arrested, Jesus proclaimed that "now is the judgment of this world: now shall the prince of this world be cast out" (John 12:31). He told them if He went upon the cross, Satan would be defeated. Satan's defeat is not in the future; it is in the past, at the cross.

In John 16:7-10 Jesus tells us that when He departs He will send the Holy Spirit to reside with us, and that one of the tasks of this Spirit of God is to convince the world that the prince of the world, Satan, is already defeated and judged. His power over the believer is broken *as long as we remain in full faith.*

Imprisoned at Armageddon

While Satan yet remains in the earth, directing sinners and tempting believers—looking for new converts—and still possesses access to heaven, the Apostle John tells us of his future sentence.

In Rev. 12:7-11, John describes a vision God gave him of future events. The vision is of Satan and all his army of fallen angels being cast out of heaven for the last time and being denied access to the throne of God. This will occur at the midpoint of the seven-year tribulation period, and an enraged Satan will create havoc in the earth bringing about the Battle of Armageddon and the near-annihilation of the human race.

> And there was a war in heaven: Michael and his angels fought against the dragon; and the dragon fought and his angels, And prevailed not; neither was there place found any more in heaven. And the great dragon was cast out, that old serpent, called the Devil, and Satan, which deceiveth the whole world: he was cast out into the earth, and his angels were cast out with him. And I heard a loud voice saying in heaven, Now is come salvation, and strength, and the kingdom of our God, and the power of his Christ: for the accuser of our brethren is cast down, which accused them before our God day and night. (Rev. 12:7-11)

181

During the Battle of Armageddon at the end of the Great Tribulation, Satan will lead his army and evil armies of the earth into battle against Christ and His forces. The spiritual powers of good and evil will be entwined so completely in the earthly powers that they will become unified—incarnate.

Jesus, of course, is overwhelmingly victorious, and Satan is cast into a bottomless pit, where he resides for 1000 years as Jesus reigns on earth.

> And I saw an angel come down from heaven, having the key of the bottomless pit and a great chain in his hand. And he laid hold on the dragon, that old serpent, which is the Devil, and Satan, and bound him a thousand years. And cast him into the bottomless pit, and shut him up, and set a seal upon him, that he should deceive the nations no more, till the thousand years should be fulfilled: and after that he must be loosed a little season. (Rev. 20:1-3)

Condemned Forever

After Christ's millennial reign, during which He greatly suppresses sin and notions of evil still remaining, Satan is released from the bottomless pit. The devil immediately sets about to organize the remnant of evil into an army that will encircle Jerusalem. But there is no battle. God rains fire upon the army—perhaps lightning or a forest fire, perhaps fiery brimstone; no one knows for sure. The rebelling army will be destroyed, and Satan will be cast into a lake of fire forever. Matt. 25:41 tells us this everlasting fire was "prepared for the devil and his angels."

And when the thousand years are expired, Satan shall be loosed out of his prison, And shall go out to deceive the nations which are in the four quarters of the earth, Gog and Magog, to gather them together to battle: the number of whom is as the sand of the sea. And they went up on the breadth of the earth, and compassed the camp of the saints about, and the beloved city: and fire came down from God out of heaven, and devoured them. And the devil that deceived them was cast into the lake of fire and brimstone, where the beast and the false prophet are, and shall be tormented day and night for ever and ever. (Rev. 20:7-10)

Thus ends the activities of the greatest angel ever created by God, Lucifer. Because of selfish desires he was exiled from heaven and became Satan, prince of darkness. He was judged and found guilty, and his work was annulled at the cross of Christ. He will be defeated at the Battle of Armageddon and sentenced to 1000 years in the bottomless pit, followed by an eternity in the lake of fire.

17

The most profound question that rings throughout the universe, the question that represents the greatest mystery of all, is simply, "Is God?" While much evidence exists, the most obvious proof is right before our eyes.

How to Know God Exists

The answer to the question, "Does God really exist?" is stated in all its fullness in the third chapter of Exodus where God says, "I Am" (Exod. 3:14). And that should settle it. But that is the easy way. Man has never done things the easy way; it is too confusing for his finite mind. Man would rather wade through a network of meshing, overlapping, intertwining avenues of reality to reach a destination that lies just two words away. Okay, let us wade.

Revealed Evidence

Theology leads us to three avenues through which God reveals himself to man. The first avenue of divine revelation is *revealed evidence.* God has left a witness to our spirit. It is summed up in Paul's letter to the church in Rome: "The Spirit itself beareth witness with our spirit, that we are the children of God" (Rom. 8:16). Here we see the absolute witness.

No man who has ever been witnessed to personally by God has ever denied His existence. The certainty of God's witness is summarized in the often-heard statement, "when you know you know, you know." There is no visible sign, no tangible evidence, but God in a still small voice says, "I Am."

John 4:24 says that God is a spirit, and that we must worship Him through our spirits. It is okay to explore the tangible evidence for God's existence, to help the "educated" person believe He exists, but *all* should seek this personal relationship with God on the spirit level and not the mental or intellectual level.

But let us get down to bare facts. Suppose God has never spoken to you, and you have difficulty communicating with Him at the spirit level. There is a second avenue to the realization that God exists. God has not left himself without a witness that can be grasped by every man. The Holy Bible is just that witness. The Bible is *written evidence.*

Written Evidence

If the Bible is to be accepted as "just another theory," subject to error, then it is not a witness to God's existence. Therefore the first step in understanding this witness is to inspect the Bible, and if it is found to possess characteristics far beyond human creativity, then it can be assumed that it must come from a being superior to man, that is, God. And if it has patterns of consistency, then these patterns can be pursued to understand the nature of God and man.

The most consistent quality of the Bible is truth. It is truth that sets man free (John 8:32). If one lie can be found in the Bible, then it is not from God. If Jesus did not live a sinless life, then the Bible is false. If any man can be found to be sinless, then the Bible is not a witness. These are the conclusions we reach when we inspect the Bible and its qualities: that man is a sinful being; Jesus the Son of God is sinless; the Bible reveals only truth and we can accept anything it says, based upon the context of its use, to guide us through life; that in accepting Jesus we are given eternal life with God and that by following the teachings of the Bible we can live the abundant life it promises (John 10:10). Glorious rewards are available if we believe that the Bible is what it asserts. (See chapter one, "Why the Bible Is So Amazing.")

Natural Evidence

The third avenue to the truth about God is *natural evidence.* Just as the archaeologist learns of a race of people from the discovery of its art objects, we can come to know God by studying His creations.

Rom. 1:20 tells us we can understand the invisible things (the Godhead, divine power) by observing the visible or natural things. The peace of St. Francis came from his ability to see and understand God in all of nature around him, for example, to see God's powerful design in the ability of a simple leaf to harness energy from the sun's rays and fix it upon carbon dioxide and mineral-rich water to produce a food substance that provides man with all his required sugars, starches, fats, and vitamins. Photosynthesis is a God-ordained process without which man cannot exist. Then to watch this same tree shake away its old leaves and burst forth new buds every spring, year after year without the help of anyone, is the greatest wonder of life.

Who set this process into motion? Who sustains it? Who provides the rain, the sun? Acts 14:17 says that God left a witness so that we might answer these questions. That witness is rain from heaven and fruitful seasons. These occurrences are God's witness that He exists.

Where did our planets come from? Some scientists

claim two stars nearly collided and the gravitational pull of one broke off nine large chunks of the other. These cooled and fell into an orbit. This theory has been called the *hypothesis of dynamic encounter*. But who created those stars? Who ordered the preexisting systems and laws of gravity, cooling bodies, crystallization, and orbiting bodies? Psalm 19 says by observing the heavens we see the handiwork of God, which declares His glory. Day after day, night after night, the heavens reveal the existence of God.

One of the most crowning evidences to the existence of God is the existence of man. Look at the human body. What a profound mechanism.

Our bodies have over ten thousand miles of blood vessels that carry 25 trillion red corpuscles, pushed by an organ that pulsates 40 million times a year for 70 or 80 years without a single rest.

And look at our eyes, perfect optical instruments— why do we have two? Two eyes are required to see depth, three dimensions. How else would we know if an object was getting closer and not simply larger.

Ever wonder what happens to the dust blinked out of our eyes? The eye-cleaning fluid (tears), which comes forth automatically every time we blink, collects this dust and by way of ducts transports it down into the nose, a natural filter of the lungs. Later, the dust is mechanically blown out with air from lungs that have a surface area of over 2000 square feet. The air tunnel leading to these lungs terminates into about 25 million tiny branches.

What an amazing and unique mechanism, the human body. We could go on and on about muscles, the digestive system, senses of taste, feel, and smell, how ears work, and how in just one square inch of skin there are 600 sweat glands, 100 fatty glands, over 200 inches of blood vessels, 156 inches of nerve cable, and more than three million cells, each filled with several apparati providing assorted functions. And our system of communication, bone structure, and ability to see color all attest to a divine Creator. Is it possible that all this—and much, much more—could have occurred by chance?

Who ordained the universe and called forth the earth and all its laws of nature? Do yourself a favor this week. Take a hike into the woods alone and read Psalm 104 along the way. Here is an excerpt as it reads in the beautiful language of the King James Version:

He sendeth the springs into the valleys, which run among the hills. They give drink to every beast of the field: the wild asses quench their thirst. By them shall the fowls of the heaven have their habitation, which sing among the branches. He watereth the hills from his chambers: the earth is satisfied with the fruit of thy works. He causeth the grass to grow for the cattle, and herb for the service of man: that he may bring forth food out of the earth; And wine that maketh glad the heart of man, and oil to make his face to shine, and bread which strengtheneth man's heart. The trees of the Lord are full of sap; the cedars of Lebanon, which he hath planted; Where the birds make their nests: as for the stork, the fir trees are her house. The high hills are a refuge for the wild goats; and the rocks for the conies. He appointed the moon for seasons: the sun knoweth his going down. Thou makest darkness, and it is night: wherein all the beasts of the forest do creep forth. The young lions roar after their prey, and seek their meat from God. The sun ariseth, they gather themselves together, and lay them down in their dens. Man goeth forth unto his work and to his labour until the evening. O Lord, how manifold are thy works! in wisdom hast thou made them all: The earth is full of thy riches. (verses 10-24)

In light of this and other evidence there is only one title for the one who says there is no God. This title is written in God's book, in the first sentence of the first verse of the fourteenth Psalm: "The fool hath said in his heart, There is no God."

Evidence in the Animals

In observing animal life around us we notice several phenomena which witness to an intelligent Creator, as opposed to an impersonal chain of evolution. One such witness is *instinct*.

Instinct compells a body to correct action to resolve a need in the species. For instance, while appetite *craves* food, instinct *directs* the food-gathering process, causing a body to select from the enormous diversity of foods only those nourishing to its body. In humans it seeks a blend of meats, grain products, dairy products, and vegetables. This instinct may be seen in even a simple Southern meal of cornbread and collard greens cooked in a piece of fat. The fat provides the meat protein, the cornbread provides the carbohydrates found in grains, and the collards provide the calcium of dairy products as well as offering the benefits of vegetables. In an area of Africa this same nourishment is acquired by draining a portion of blood from the veins of cattle and mixing it with milk for a completely nourishing drink. Whatever the foods, the nutritional needs of the human body are universally the same and, consequently, staples have been established by each class of people.

With honeybees, the food requirement is met in a special blend of pollen, water, and honey. In the event a hive should develop a deficit of queen bees, ordinary eggs are placed in enlarged cells and fed a copious amount of a peculiar food that transforms the common bee into a queen bee to perpetuate the hive. Neither experience nor theory could have taught the bees when or how to achieve this phenomenal trick. Surely the instinct is God-directed and is a result of careful planning from the Master Designer. To think otherwise is irrational.

The young of all species begin feeding immediately, without hesitation or decision making, upon the *proper* foods for their diet. The actions of some young instinctively urge the mother to produce a correspondent reaction. Young birds raise their heads high and open their bills. This properly executed action compels the mother to seek food just as a lactating mother is compelled to lift a crying child to her breast. Such instinctive correlation is necessary for survival.

Similar patterns are seen in animals such as squirrels, ants, and many rodents, who, without being taught, instinctively harvest, dry, and store the exact amount and species of seeds, hay, or nuts to provide a continuation of food through a snowy winter.

Instinct also manifests itself in the building habits of social animals and insects—most of which surpass in design and detail all that the most intelligent human planning can achieve.

Without education from their parents, without trial

and error, without confusion and with no plan of action, honeybees proceed to build hexagonal chambers for a comb that, according to the most refined laws of geometry, yields the greatest amount of individual cell space using the least amount of materials and labor and provides maximum strength to sustain the immense weight of the honey and the young brood. For centuries this exact structure, the perfect habitat, has been constructed in the precise manner as set forth by the Creator of the bee. There has been no evolutionary development or improvements made upon the bee hive.

Likewise, since the dawn of history ornithologists have known the bird by the nest it builds. If you take a hundred species of young birds and release them in a forest where they have no contact with adults of their species, each bird, without hesitation, will seek out the same materials used by its predecessors to build a nest exactly like one which it has never seen before. A hundred species will build a hundred different nests while a thousand birds of the same species will build the exact same nest evidencing that a superior Creator has programed each species with an instinctive nature that provides them with the proper and most perfect abode for nesting.

Similar examples can be found in the multichambered tunnels of ants and termites, in the building of strong dams by beavers, in the nests of wasps, and in the netting traps of spiders. An even greater phenomenon can be seen in the action of a butterfly which provides food for its soon-to-hatch larvae. The food for the larvae is entirely different from the butterfly's own diet, yet very nourishing to the larvae, a worm which the butterfly has never seen and never will see. How does the butterfly know the diet of its young (for it will die long before the young hatches) if not preprogramed by its Creator.

One particular wasp, the potter's wasp, has the innate ability to insert its stinger like a surgeon's scalpel into the backs of caterpillars to the exact depth that reaches the nervous system, in order to inject a special fluid that paralyzes the caterpillar without killing him. The wasp then entombs the live and motionless caterpillar in a clay chamber containing eggs of its young. Many days later, long after the adult wasp is dead, the eggs will hatch and feed upon the fresh caterpillar before emerging from the small clay pot.

Such an action is necessary for the continuance of the species of the potter's wasp. Yet the action, knowing exactly the right spot to sting to cause paralysis, and knowing how to entomb the victim, is not a result of trial and error but an instinct placed by the hand of God.

It is the same survival instinct that causes certain birds to make their way over land and sea, sometimes thousands of miles night and day, to seek out the same nesting grounds year after year. The same survival instinct that causes certain species of fish to journey far from their usual haunts, where would seem to be the most likely place to breed, to plant eggs in shallow inland streams to provide the proper environment for the hatching young it will never see. The same inbred action exists in the plant kingdom, as witnessed by the wounded dogwood tree, which expends its stored energy to flush out a double portion of blossoms in a final attempt to perpetuate its species.

Surely it is obvious that these examples are only a few of the hundreds that attest to a degree of survival that goes beyond function or mere existence, and witnesses to a carefully planned creation from a concerned Creator.

Instinct delays not; it makes no mistakes; it never falters. In the words of the eighteenth-century philosopher Kant, "It is the voice of God."

Evidence from Our Environment

Before resting the case whereby we show the existence of God by studying His works, we must look at His inanimate world. The atmosphere, for instance, is an ocean of air God has placed us in for our comfort and protection. This thin ocean is about forty-five miles deep and is held down by gravity. It contains the proper proportions of gases, uniform everywhere, that are necessary for both plant and animal life—thin enough to allow rapid movement, yet thick enough to sustain heavy aircraft and the flight of birds.

God has made the atmosphere nearly transparent, so as not to impair our vision. Yet he has filled it with billions of tiny particles that glow in the sunlight, illuminating our world with what we call daylight. This phenomenon allows us to see in shadows and inside our homes. On the moon, where there is no atmosphere, astronauts must be careful when walking in their shadows, for it is absolutely black and renders the treacherous terrain invisible.

Not only does the atmosphere scatter the bright rays of the sun, but it captures and diffuses its immense heat. If God had not provided this protective cloak, we would burn up in the direct sun and freeze in the shadows. After the atmosphere has absorbed the heat of the day, it releases it in the cool of the night, to keep our temperature extremes in a comfortable, livable range. Air currents carry the warm air around the globe, to maintain a relatively consistent temperature everywhere.

God in His immense knowledge has also provided the earth and all its inhabitants with abundant water, a material that will easily vaporize into clouds, drift around the globe, and shower the thirsty lands. The moisture in the soil then dissolves natural mineral fertilizers and carries them into plants, which provide food and shelter for the world. Excess rains trek along the myriad crevices and streams in an immense network that delivers the water from the watershed back to the oceans and lakes, where the cycle repeats. In this manner God keeps His land refreshed, while providing for His organic creations.

As most materials cool they become more dense and heavier, but with water God changed His law. As water freezes it expands and becomes lighter, causing it to float. Thank God for this.

In the winter the surface of a lake freezes over, providing a protective blanket for the aquatic life below. If ice sank to the bottom, the entire lake would eventually become a solid block of ice that even the hottest summers could not melt. Not only would our fresh water resources lose their lives, but the lakes could no longer serve as reservoirs for the water cycle. And more importantly, soil moisture would also freeze in the root zone, killing off all perennial forms of plant life. Animal life under these circumstances would be most difficult and eventually impossible. God knew this from the beginning when He harmonized the elements of the universe, when He established order and balance among His organic and inorganic creations.

Evidence in Patterns

The patterns and laws of uniformity used by God in

constructing the universe and every atom in it, when closely analyzed, become overwhelmingly impressive. The hairs upon our heads display an intricate spiral pattern, starting from one point upon the peak of the crown sometimes called "the cowlick." This same pattern is duplicated in the placement of seeds in the head of the sunflower and in the spiraling of a pine cone.

One particular mathematical pattern has an astonishing correspondent application. The leaves of plants are arranged in spirals about the stem. There exists a definite ratio between the number of leaves to each turn around the stem. If we studied a great number of plants and wrote out these ratios we would discover the following series:

$$\frac{\text{turns}}{\text{Leaves}} = \frac{1}{2} \quad \frac{1}{3} \quad \frac{2}{5} \quad \frac{3}{8} \quad \frac{5}{13} \quad \frac{8}{21} \quad \frac{13}{34}$$

The mathematical explanation of this series is simple. The denominators (lower numerals) of any two adjacent numbers, when added, become the denominator of the next number (2+3=5, 3+5=8, etc.). And the denominator of any number is the sum of its numerator (upper numeral) and the denominator of the preceding number (3=1+2, 5=2+3, etc.).

If we inspect the *periodic times* of the planets, the time required for a planet to orbit the sun, we can write out their ratio relationships. Starting with the distant planets, we discover Uranus has a periodic time about 1/2 that of Neptune. Coming closer to the sun, we notice the following: Saturn is 1/3 that of Uranus, Jupiter 2/5 that of Saturn, the asteroids (cluster of small planets between Mars and Jupiter) 3/8 that of Jupiter, Mars 5/13 that of the asteroids, Venus 8/21 that of Mars, and

Mercury, the planet closest to the sun, 13/24 that of Venus. The earth's periodic time does not fit into the pattern. This series is 1/2, 1/3, 2/5, 3/8, 5/13, 8/21, 13/24. God used the same pattern of relationship on the periodic times of the great planets as he did on the delicate leaves that dance around a twig.

The fact that these and other laws of nature are subject to mathematical explanation are evidence that the universe is constructed by a superior intelligent being. Can we doubt the harmony God has established in the universe after observing such astronomical duplications?

Nature all around us proclaims God in His infinite wisdom and design abilities. Even the moral nature of man links Him with an undefined moral system created by God.

Morality in man is an instilled sense of duty directly attached to happiness. We did not develop or reason morality, rather it was programed in us. We quite naturally feel obligated to moral law. Beyond a quest for our own happiness, we morally seek happiness for others.

Men and women of all races, ages, and lands have always presumed a God and sought some form of worship of this higher creative intelligence. That "God is" is the only rational solution.

I live only five minutes from the Gulf of Mexico and often take my family to sit on the sand late in the afternoon to watch the sun set in the ocean. This is a sight very few Americans get to see unless they live on the West Coast of America or Florida. What a magnificent spectacle. As the large, orange sun drops below the razor-edge horizon of the reflecting ocean, we can actually see it moving. Or more accurately, knowing the sun is a relatively fixed point, we can actually feel the earth rotating beneath our feet. The grandiose and unbelievable mechanism necessary for the earth to revolve is humanly incomprehensible. Whenever I see this awesome sight I think of the opening lines of a favorite hymn.

Oh Lord my God! When I in awesome wonder
Consider all the worlds Thy hands have made,
I see the stars, I hear the rolling thunder,
Thy power throughout the universe displayed,

When through the woods and forest glades I wander
And hear the birds sing sweetly in the trees,
When I look down from lofty mountain grandeur
And hear the brook and feel the gentle breeze,

Then sings my soul, my Savior God to Thee;
How great Thou art! How great Thou art!
Then sings my soul, my Savior God to Thee;
How great Thou art! How great Thou art!

18

Did you ever wonder what heaven is like or where it is? Is it simply a spiritual state of mind, or is it a place with people, trees, animals, streets, and law and order?

Is Heaven a Real Place?

The author Henry David Thoreau was once quoted as saying heaven is not only above your head but below your feet. But the author God, in His famous best seller *The Holy Bible*, tells us an entirely different story. Now, we are given a wonderful gift called *free will* that allows us to believe whichever author we wish, the author of *Walden's Pond* or the author of the universe. Let's see what this second author says about heaven.

What Heaven Looks Like

The Bible doesn't tell us how large all of heaven is, but in Revelation 21, the Apostle John prophetically sees one of its cities and describes it. This city is filled with the glistening radiance of God's glory and is surrounded by a broad, high wall through which twelve gates open, three each on the north, east, south, and west sides. An angel stands before each gate. The wall is massive. It stands over 300 feet tall, and upon the walls are twelve beautiful fountains garnished in precious stones.

The city is cube-shaped and very large. Its dimensions measure 1500 miles on each side, two-thirds the size of the United States. This city is made of a pure transparent gold. The gates are made of a special pearl and are always open. There is never any darkness because of the presence of our Lord. Jesus said, "I am the light." No immoral or evil person will ever enter this particular city.

In verse 27 we discover who lives there, "they which are written in the Lamb's book of Life." God has a throne there, but His Temple is located elsewhere, perhaps in another city.

In Chapter 22 we read more detail. Down the main street flows a river of crystal-pure water, bordered by trees that produce a new crop every month.

Now read something very special:

> And he said unto me, These sayings are faithful and true: and the Lord God of the holy prophets sent his angel to shew unto his servants the things which must shortly be done. Behold, I come quickly: blessed is he that keepeth the sayings of the prophecy of this book. (Rev. 22:6-7)

God says this description is true and those who have the faith to believe it will receive a special blessing. He has sent His angel to John to record this vision *especially for Christians.* Isn't that exciting!

Where Heaven Is Located

Heaven is definitely *up.* Deut. 26:15 says, "Look down from thy holy habitation, from heaven." This means heaven is away from our earth. It is out of our solar system, away from any sun.

> And the city had no need of the sun, neither of the moon, to shine in it: for the glory of God did lighten it, and the Lamb is the light thereof. (Rev. 21:23)

Heaven is not far away, however, for angels daily scoot

back and forth between heaven and earth (John 1:51).
What is very important is that heaven is *not* a spiritual
state of being, nor an eternal resting spot in the ground,
but a *real place* somewhere away from here. Read carefully this most encouraging and reassuring statement
made by Jesus to His followers.

Let not your heart be troubled: ye believe in God,
believe also in me. In my Father's house are many
mansions: if it were not so, I would have told you. I
go to prepare a place for you. And if I go and prepare
a place for you, I will come again, and receive you
unto myself: that where I am there ye may be also.
And whither I go ye know, and the way ye know.
(John 14:1-4)

These words come to us directly from Jesus. He is saying, "Christians, don't worry about death. The way to
heaven is to believe in me the way you believe in God.
Heaven is not filled with spiritual cubbyholes but glorious dwellings—mansions—built for people. I'm going
now to prepare a place for you." Then he closes by prom-
ising to take every Christian to this wonderful place:
"the way ye know." Jesus has said, "I am the way." Read
this passage over and over then trouble no more.

Some Christian astronomers tell us there is a vast hole
in our universe in the midst of the constellation Orion
in the northern sky where there are no stars to be seen. It
is their belief that through this hole the Holy City
described above will descend to the earth sometime in
the future. Support for this theory is found in the
following passages.

And I John saw the holy city, new Jerusalem, coming
down from God out of heaven, prepared as a bride

adorned for her husband. And I heard a great voice out of heaven saying, Behold, the tabernacle of God is with men, and he will dwell with them, and they shall be his people, and God himself shall be with them, and be their God. (Rev. 21:2-3)

For thou hast said in thine heart, I will ascend into heaven, I will exalt my throne above the stars of God: I will sit also upon the mount of congregation, in the sides of the north. (Isa. 14:13)

He stretched out the north over the empty place, and hangeth the earth upon nothing. (Job 26:7)

Beautiful for situation, the joy of the whole earth, is mount Zion, on the sides of the north, the city of the great King. (Ps. 48:2)

For promotion cometh neither from the east, nor from the west, nor from the south. (Ps. 75:6)

These references all seem to indicate that heaven is not everywhere, but in a particular location—in the direction of the northern sky.

Material Things In Heaven

Not only does the Bible treat heaven as if it were a particular place in a specific location, but it also tells of material things there. We have already read of mansions, streets, rivers, and trees. In Rev. 5:1 we read, "And I saw in the right hand of him that set on the *throne a book*." In Luke 22:30 there is reference to *eating* and *drinking*; in Dan. 7:9 to *clothes*, in Rev. 15:7 to *vials*; and in Rev. 5:8 and 8:2 to *musical instruments*.

Gen. 1:1 tells us that not only earth but heaven too

was *created* by God. In Col. 1:16 we read that God also created "things" for both earth and heaven. And that some of these things are visible (books, food, trees) while others are invisible (powers, principalities, etc.). Yes, heaven is a real *place*, full of material *things*, all created for His pleasure (Rev. 4:11).

Who Lives in Heaven?

God says heaven is now inhabited by a numberless quantity of heavenly hosts (Jer. 33:22). Even the angels there are innumerable (Heb. 12:22). These heavenly hosts live in dominions or principalities (Eph. 3:9-10), that is, specific areas or cities governed by laws or ordinances (Jer. 31:35-36). Heaven is God's kingdom, and He has a temple there. There is an army too (Dan. 4:35). Heaven is not a place absent of wars. Isa. 14:12-14 tells us heaven was once invaded by Lucifer, who was cut down for his rebellion. Jesus, in Luke 10:17-19, tells seventy of His followers that He witnessed this battle. And in Rev. 12:7-9, John prophetically catches a glimpse of a second war that is yet to occur. During this second war Michael and an army of angels will fight Satan and his host of fallen angels. Satan still has access to heaven, now. But after this second battle he will be cast to the earth, never to return.

There are physical bodies in heaven. At least three people went to heaven in their physical bodies: Jesus (Luke 24:39), Elijah (2 Kings 2:11), and Enoch (Gen. 5:24). Elijah and Enoch never died but went straight to heaven in their natural bodies. They are examples of being *raptured*. Jesus went to heaven in a resurrected body that has the same appearance as His earthly body (Zech. 12:10). All Christians who have entered through death are also in heaven with our Lord, right now. Man with his very limited mind often sees death as tragic and says, "Why, Why, Why?" But God assures us that "to die is gain" (Phil. 1:21-23).

Many say there are no animals in heaven, but the Bible has several references to horses in heaven (2 Kings 2:11-12; 6:17; Zech. 1:8; 6:1-5; Rev. 6:1-8; 19:11). Many say animals have no spirits. That makes it impossible for animals to know God, but does it keep them out of heaven? Trees are alive and do not have spirits, yet they are in heaven. I believe heaven is full of the wonderful things on earth that give us joy—dogs, cats, beautiful flying birds.

"Has any man ever seen heaven?" The Bible says yes. At least six men in the Bible saw heaven before they died: Ezekiel (Ezek. 1:1), Jesus (Mark 1:10), Nathaniel (John 1:51), Stephen (Acts 7:56), Peter (Acts 10:11), and John (Rev. 4:1).

The Road to Heaven

Now here is the most important question of all: "How can we get to heaven?" Earth is not our home; heaven is (Heb. 13:14). Psalm 15 tells us who will dwell in God's house.

Lord, who shall abide in thy tabernacle? who shall dwell in thy holy hill? He that walketh uprightly, and worketh righteousness, and speaketh the truth in his heart. He that backbiteth not with his tongue, nor doeth evil to his neighbour, nor taketh up a reproach against his neighbour. In whose eyes a vile person is contemned; but he honoureth them that fear the Lord. He that sweareth to his own hurt and changeth not. He that putteth not out his money to usury, nor taketh reward against the innocent. He that doeth these things shall never be moved.

John 3:16 tells us who will be given eternal life with our Lord. Read it. In John 14:5-6 Thomas asks our Lord how will we know the way to heaven? Jesus answered, "I am the way . . . no man cometh unto the Father, but by me." Jesus is the way to heaven. *Follow Him.*

God says heaven is a real place located outside our solar system, with real people, angels, material things, a social order, temporary angelic conflict, eternal peace and joy, mansions, and singing. Jesus is there now (not here as some think) and has a place prepared and waiting for every Christian. Can we believe Him, the One who made us and all the earth?

PART FIVE

THE TIME OF THE END

19

We know our age will someday come to an end, but we don't know when. Yet the Bible gives signs that inform us the time is near. Current events give clues to . . .

How Near Are We to the End?

One of the reasons we know the Bible is from God is that time and again predictions are made that come true exactly as they were made, sometimes thousands of years later. This phenomenon is called fulfilled prophecy.

Since we know the Bible gives us the complete history of mankind on earth, from beginning to end, we can look for predictions or prophecies of events that will occur just prior to the rapture and the tribulation period. If we see these prophecies being fulfilled, we can assume the time of Christ's second coming is near.

During the first century, which included Jesus' first entry into our world, numerous prophecies were fulfilled. These became a sign to the Jews that the Messiah had come. For the next 1800 years almost no prophecies were fulfilled. This was the period when the Christian church and the message of salvation through Christ was preached throughout the world.

Then at the turn of the twentieth century, fulfillment of ancient prophecies again began to occur. First a few, then many. The church has become excited, for these prophecies are those which mark the end of our present age and the return of our Lord. Following are twelve of the most prominent prophecies fulfilled since 1900 that tell us the end of the age is at hand.

Spiritual Revival Predicted

Often it has been said that we can lay the New Testament over the Old Testament and that the physical events of the Old Testament are repeated in the spiritual events of the New Testament. The Old Testament events are called "types." By coordinating these types with the prophecies we can more easily get to the revelation.

In Joel 2:28-31, the prophet says there will be a great outpouring of God's Holy Spirit upon mankind before the day of the Lord shall come. In the Old Testament this pouring down of the Spirit for spiritual food is typified (shown in a type) by God pouring rain upon Israel to provide physical food.

There were two periods of rain in Judea. In November, God sent the early rains to soften the dry ground for seed planting. In April, He sent the latter rains to swell the kernels of wheat and barley for harvesting. In the spiritual dispensation of the New Testament God poured the early rains of His Spirit upon Peter and the early church leaders to give them power to plant the seed of the Christian church. The next 1800 years marked the period of a growing crop, nourishing the Christian church to fruition. Today we again see the Spirit of God being poured upon mankind in the same manner as occurred on the day of Pentecost in Jerusalem. God has provided two physical rains to nourish our bodies and two spiritual outpourings to nourish our spirits in preparation for the first and second coming of Jesus—the planting of the crop and the harvesting of its fruit.

The day of Pentecost was marked with bold preaching and the granting of "gifts" to believers. This story is recorded in the second chapter of Acts. Miracles and the conversion of thousands were prominent on that day. If these phenomena marked the first spiritual outpouring, we can expect them to mark the second also.

In 1866, Michael Baxter, founder of the *Christian Herald*, wrote, "increased faith to work miracles and unparalleled boldness in preaching of the gospel will characterize the coming outpouring of the Spirit. . . . But this end is not yet attained; therefore these gifts cannot altogether have ceased, or been entirely withdrawn, although they have been suspended and temporarily withdrawn as a mark of displeasure for the apostatising of the church from her first love."

Just a few years later the showers of the latter rains began to trickle. By the 1950s the rains began to pour. Throughout the '60s and '70s every major denomination had at least been dampened, and most inundated, by the pouring out of God's love upon His people. Never before since the initiation of the church on the day of Pentecost has the world seen such a splendid move of God through His people. Powerful sermons, thousands of conversions, miracles, teaching ministries, and bold witnessing are all evidence that we are in the days of the latter rains.

The most unique factor of this revival is that it bears no human leader like the revivals of Wesley and Calvin. It is God's Holy Spirit empowering His church for the day of the harvest when Jesus comes for His crop, the Christian church. The latter rains are a sign the harvest time is near.

Israel Will Go Home

In A.D. 70 Rome destroyed Jerusalem and dispersed the Jews, just as Jesus had predicted in Luke 19:43-44. The Jews remained a nation without a nation for nearly 1900 years—a miracle itself. But God said the nation of Israel would be built up before the Lord would appear (Ps. 102:16), and Isaiah prophesied "in that day" God would gather Israel from the four corners of the earth and place them under their own flag (Isa. 11:11-12).

Ezekiel's vision of the dry bones reuniting (shin bone connected to the knee bone, etc.) is explained as the nation of Israel rising like dry bones from around the world to return to their homeland (Ezek. 37:1-11).

In 1948 these prophecies were fulfilled. Israel went home and raised a flag and made miraculous recoveries, such as the Six Day War of 1967. All the events surrounding the end times has the Jews in their homeland, Israel. Now they are there, and firmly established.

Christians Hated and Killed

Jesus gives this sign in Matt. 24:9. We don't see it in America, but Underground Evangelism, Inc., reports that Christians are killed daily in Albania, Russia, and Bulgaria if caught with a Bible. They are hated and persecuted in Yugoslavia, Hungary, China, Czechoslovakia, and numerous other countries. There are only seven legal Christian churches in Russia. Theologian Dr. J. Barton Payne reports that since the 1900s there have been more people killed (martyred) for the cause of Christ than in *any previous period* of church history, including the first century. We are seeing this prophecy fulfilled now.

World Wars

In Matt. 24:7 Jesus said in the days just prior to His return nations and kingdoms would rise against each other. This world of ours had its first "world war" of the scale Jesus was talking about in 1914 and another in 1939. These wars involved all-out, hot war among the great nations of France, Great Britain, Russia, the United States, Italy, Japan, Germany, Austria-Hungary, and several others. The whole world was affected, as it is even today from the cold war, the Viet Nam War and the prophesied disturbance in the Middle East. Until the twentieth century there were no *world* wars. World wars are yet another sign of the coming of our Lord.

Pestilences

In the same Scripture Jesus prophesies pestilence, what Webster's dictionary defines as, "anything, as a doctrine, regarded as harmful or dangerous." Surely atheistic Communism, infiltrating the world like a cancer, fulfills this prophecy. Add to this the assorted sects and brotherhood philosophies pinching the Christian doctrine of free countries, and we have a catastrophic pestilence, another end-time prophecy being fulfilled.

Earthquakes

Also in Matt. 24:7 Jesus speaks of increased earthquakes just prior to His return. Here is the record of serious earthquakes over the past several hundred years:

    15th century—115
    16th century—253
    17th century—378
    18th century—640
    19th century—2119

And look at the major quakes since 1900. In 1906, San Francisco was nearly destroyed. In 1908, 75,000 died in a quake in Messina, Italy. In 1920, 180,000 died in a quake in Kansu, China. In 1943, an earthquake totally destroyed Tokyo, Japan, and 143,000 people. And there have been others of major proportions more recently in India, Guatemala, Turkey, Greece, and America. Read what the September 16, 1974, issue of *Newsweek* magazine stated: "As the planets move into alignment in 1982, their gravitational pull may cause huge storms on the sun. These storms could alter wind directions on earth, reducing the speed of the planet's rotation and triggering serious earthquakes." More major earthquakes are sure to come as the end of the age approaches.

Famines

In the same Scripture Jesus lists starvation as yet another sign of the end of the age. The world has never seen hunger such as it has in the last two decades. For the first time ever, all the nations of the world met in Rome in 1974 to determine who was hungry and why. This World Food Conference concluded that half the human race was deficient in protein; that 450 million were permanently hungry due to serious calorie deficiencies; that 100 countries were hungry, with 33 of these being designated MSA (most seriously affected); and that 10,000 to 12,000 people die every day from simple starvation. Sad figures, but another sign of the shortness of time.

Demonology Rampant

In 1 Tim. 4:1-3 we are given four more signs of the latter days. The first is a surge in the ancient and medieval practice of Satanic worship. Across America and around the world there is an increasing number of reports of demon possession, exorcism, Satanic churches, baby sacrifices, and use of hallucinogenic drugs. Public schools that do not permit Christian courses are openly teaching ESP, parapsychology, and other biblically condemned subjects.

Conscience Seared

In the same passage we are told of the "permissive society" we call ourselves today, the society that advocates the "do your own thing" philosophy without responding to the safety valve/warning system God has given us— our conscience. It has been concluded in a thesis on morality that because of a seared conscience the world morality today has reached an all-time low—the same low that prevailed in the world when Jesus made his *first* appearance. Coincidental?

Forbidding to Marry

Here is the third sign from the same 1 Timothy verse. Little need be said except that God ordained marriage and expected wise men and women to enter into this triangular covenant between God and the couple. For the couples who leave God out, there results a broken home. Because there have been so many doing this in the world today, the trend is to "live together" out of wedlock, an explosive and dangerous practice. This is surely another sign of the nearness of the second coming of Jesus. U.S. census figures for 1977 reveal 1.3 million unwed couples who were living together. The number had doubled since 1970.

Increased Vegetarian Diets

The fourth prophecy of 1 Timothy 4 tells the trend to abstain from meats. Major church groups, diet groups, back-to-earth movements, and health kickers advocate this today. The World Food Conference reports there *is* enough food (meat and vegetables) available to feed the whole world, but certain greedy countries are not allocating it properly. And doesn't it make sense that the God who made us all would also make the necessary resources to provide for us? God created animals to be eaten by man (Gen. 9:3).

Travel and Knowledge Increased

Daniel was told that his prophecies would not be understood until the end times, when travel and knowledge would be greatly increased (Dan. 12:4).

My granddad, as a boy, traveled in a horse and buggy, much like Pharaoh's chariot in 1500 B.C. You see? No increase in travel for 3400 years. Then after 1900 came the combustion engine, autos, trains, planes, then jets, rockets, and now manned outerspace vehicles—all in one lifetime. "Many shall run to and fro."

Since the 1900s knowledge and understanding, especially in science and human behavior, has increased a hundredfold over all the combined knowledge since the birth of man.

The signs of the times indicate we are in the end times, the period of Jesus' second coming. Daily we should say, "If Jesus returns today, is my life in order?"

20

*The heart of man longs to know his own destiny—
what the future holds for himself, his race, and his
land. The answers to these questions can be found
in God's message to man. The Bible gives us . . .*

A Description of the End of Time

The Bible teaches that the age we live in will someday
come to an end, and a new age will begin (Matt. 24:35).
There are over 500 prophecies given in the Bible about
the second coming of Christ, which marks the end of our
present age. Many have already come true, and others
are being fulfilled rapidly in our day. The end time marks
the end of this earthly age, *not the end of the earth.*

Here now is a summary of events as it is most popularly
believed they will occur.

Rapture

The Rapture will mark the beginning of the end. While
the word *rapture* does not appear in the Bible any more
than *Easter* or *Christmas*, its occurrence is just as sure.
The rapture is that time when the bodies of all deceased
Christians will join their soul and spirit. At that time
Christ will appear in the clouds and remove His church
(living Christians) from the world, leaving behind a world
of unbelievers. Read how Paul describes the rapture in
1 Thess. 4:13-18:

> But I would not have you to be ignorant, brethren,
> concerning them which are asleep, that ye sorrow
> not, even as others which have no hope. For if we

believe that Jesus died and rose again, even so them also which sleep in Jesus will God bring with him. For this we say unto you by the word of the Lord, that we which are alive and remain unto the coming of the Lord shall not prevent them which are asleep. For the Lord himself shall descend from heaven with a shout, with the voice of the archangel, and with the trump of God: and the dead in Christ shall rise first: Then we which are alive and remain shall be caught up together with them in the clouds, to meet the Lord in the air: and so shall we ever be with the Lord. Wherefore comfort one another with these words.

What a blessing this Scripture carries for the believer. Life does not end with death. This doctrine, which Paul received directly from Christ ("by the word of the Lord"), is not confined to the letter Paul wrote to the church at Thessalonica in A.D. 52, his very first letter. It continues to be a part of the Christian doctrine he delivers from city to city as he establishes churches. In A.D. 57 Paul wrote the church at Corinth near Athens, Greece, telling them also about the rapture:

Behold, I shew you a mystery; We shall not all sleep, but we shall be changed. In a moment, in the twinkling of an eye, at the last trump: for the trumpet shall sound, and the dead shall be raised incorruptible, and we shall be changed. For this corruptible must put on incorruption, and this mortal must put on immortality. (1 Cor. 15:51-53)

If we need further proof that this doctrine is sound and that it comes from the Lord, we can read what Jesus told

218

His followers in A.D. 30 about the end of the age and rapture:

> And as he sat upon the mount of Olives, the disciples came unto him privately, saying, Tell us, when shall these things be? and what shall be the sign of thy coming, and of the end of the world? (Matt. 24:3)

> Then shall two be in the field; the one shall be taken, and the other left. . . . Watch therefore: for ye know not what hour your Lord doth come. (Matt. 24:40-42)

Jesus tells us that some will be raptured, some will not. For God has not chosen to pour out His anger upon us, but to save us through Christ; He died for us so that we can live with Him forever, whether we are dead or alive at the time of His return (1 Thess. 5:9-10).

At the rapture of the saints, Christ does not set foot on earth, but is merely seen in the clouds, then disappears with His church for seven years.

The Great Tribulation

The name given to the seven-year period following rapture, in which God pours judgment upon an evil world, is the *great tribulation*. In Matt. 24:21-22 Jesus describes the horror on earth during this period:

> For then shall be great tribulation, such as was not since the beginning of the world to this time, no, nor ever shall be. And except those days should be shortened, there should no flesh be saved: but for the elect's sake those days shall be shortened.

Even in the Old Testament book of Daniel we read this prophecy about the tribulation period:

And at that time shall Michael stand up, the great prince which standeth for the children of thy people: and there shall be a time of trouble, such as never was since there was a nation even to that same time: and at that time thy people shall be delivered, every one that shall be found written in the book. (Dan. 12:1)

The Apostle John, while exiled on the Island of Patmos off the coast of Turkey in A.D. 96, was permitted to prophetically see all the gory details of the great tribulation period. These are described in Revelation 12-19.

The Antichrist
Paul the Apostle in his second letter to the church at Thessalonica said:

Let no man deceive you by any means: for that day shall not come, except there come a falling away first, and that man of sin be revealed, the son of perdition; Who opposeth and exalteth himself above all that is called God, or that is worshipped; so that he as God sitteth in the temple of God, shewing himself that he is God. Remember ye not, that, when I was yet with you, I told you of these things? (2 Thess. 2:3-5)

The *Antichrist* is the name given to the dictator who will be in control over the world during the seven-year tribulation period. He is given a symbolic representation in Rev. 13:1. Read carefully what John says about this person, pictured here as a beast:

And I stood upon the sand of the sea, and saw a beast rise up out of the sea [he sees a dictator rise to take

220

over the world], having seven heads and ten horns, and upon his horns ten crowns, and upon his heads the name of blasphemy.

The seven heads are explained in Revelation 17 as the seven kingdoms that hold Israel in bondage throughout our present age. History tells us the first five were Chaldea, Egypt, Babylon, Medo-Persia, and Greece. And at the time of John's writing, Rome ruled over them.

And there are seven kings: five are fallen, and one is, and the other is not yet come; and when he cometh, he must continue a short space. (Rev. 17:10)

In A.D. 70 Jerusalem was destroyed under the Roman rule, and the Jewish nation was dispersed. For 1900 years the Jews wandered without a land. But in 1948 Israel went home, and today they rule themselves in their own land. This prophecy in Revelation says there will be one more dictator over Israel, but his reign will be short. It refers to the reign of the Antichrist during the tribulation period.

The ten horns with ten crowns represent ten nations united with great power. (Many believe this will be the powerful European Common Market.) These ten nations will sign a treaty giving their power and strength to the Antichrist, dictator of the seventh kingdom ruling most of the world.

And the ten horns which thou sawest are ten kings, which have received no kingdom as yet; but receive power as kings one hour with the beast. These have one mind, and shall give their power and strength unto the beast. (Rev. 17:12-13)

221

It is also important to note that the dragon of Rev. 13:2 is Satan, who gives supernatural powers to the Antichrist. The Antichrist will be a powerful man.

The False Prophet

The False Prophet will also support the Antichrist. He is the religious leader of the World Church, a union of major denominations who cling to a religion based upon brotherhood and not upon Christ. In Rev. 13:11-13 John sees the False Prophet as another beast coming out of the earth (he is named in Rev. 19:20). This great religious leader will be able to perform miracles, such as making fire flame down to earth from the skies while everyone is watching. He will require the world to worship the Antichrist as God. Just as John the Baptist announced Jesus to the world, the False Prophet will announce the Antichrist.

During the first three and one-half years of the tribulation period there will be peace and false security. The Antichrist will piece the world together with miraculous maneuvers during a time of great trouble. All the world will honor him and worship him.

The Seven Seals

In Revelation 6 we read of the events of the first three and one-half years. The first four seals are the four horsemen, who represent: the Antichrist bringing peace, Russia bringing war upon Israel and Egypt, famine sweeping across the land, and death to millions brought about by the war and famine. The fifth seal represents persecution to the thousands who accept Christ after the rapture. Most will be killed. The sixth seal of destruction is brought about by some physical change in the earth that causes great earthquakes.

144,000 Witnesses

Just before John sees the breaking of the sixth seal in his vision of the end times, God ordains 144,000 Jews to be evangelists (Rev. 7:4). They are supernaturally protected from the government of the Antichrist, and their preaching brings thousands into Christianity. These thousands are of course martyred for their belief (7:9-14).

Jesus gives us this view of wars, famines, and earthquakes, as well as the preaching of the 144,000, in Matt. 24:6-14.

Then the seventh seal is broken, and there is silence in heaven for half an hour.

Abomination of Desecration

At the midpoint of the tribulation, as peace fades and the Russian war begins to develop, there is a great explosion of lightning and earthquakes on the earth. The Antichrist goes to Israel, enters the sacred Temple (Israel already has plans to build that Temple), and sits upon the throne and claims to be God (Matt. 24:15-21). Read of this account where the world worships the Antichrist also in Dan. 9:27 and Rev. 13:5-8.

Mark of the Beast

Citizens of the new dictatorship will be required to have a mark placed on their hand or forehead with a mysterious numerical value of 666. All who refuse the mark (those who refuse to worship the Antichrist) will not be given employment nor allowed to buy in any store (Rev. 13:16-18).

Last Three and One-Half Years

During the second half of the tribulation much wrath is poured upon the earth: fire, falling meteors, more earthquakes, rivers of blood, hail, cities crumbling. These catastrophes are described as the seven trumpet judgments beginning in Rev. 8:6, and the seven vial judgments of Revelation 16.

Battle of Armageddon

The Armageddon Plain is a huge valley in north-central Israel, and it is here that the armies of the world will meet for the final battle (Rev. 16:16-21). There will probably be a nuclear explosion, since the Bible says "islands vanished, and mountains flattened out, and . . . hailstones weighing a hundred pounds fell from the sky" (16:20-21, TLB). People will be walking corpses, flesh rotting away, eyes shriveling in their sockets, tongues decaying (Zech. 14). The battle is so fierce and mighty that Satan incarnates in the Antichrist and prepares to wage war upon Christ. The battle becomes a union of physical and spiritual warfare (Rev. 17:14). Just as mankind is on the brink of annihilating itself, Jesus arrives.

The Second Coming

Rev. 19:11-21 describes the entry of Jesus as seen in the vision of John the Apostle. It describes Christ and the armies of heaven, and the Antichrist mustering the remaining governments of the world to do battle against Christ. The defeat is swift. The entire army of the Antichrist is destroyed, and he and the False Prophet are thrown into a lake of fire.

An angel binds Satan and throws him in a bottomless pit for a thousand years. Jesus' own account of His second coming is given beginning in Matt. 24:30. And in 24:33 He says, "When ye shall see all these things, know that it is near, even at the doors."

The Millennial Reign

After the great battle of Armageddon there are many months of cleaning up the land for the remaining people. A vast grave is dug east of the Dead Sea for burial (Ezek. 39:9-16). Jesus rules on the earth with the believers for a thousand years (Rev. 20:4).

In Summary

The events surrounding the close of this age begin with the rapture, the supernatural removal of all Christians, living and dead, from the earth to join Christ in heaven. The rapture is followed by a seven-year tribulation period that begins with world peace brought about by the deceptive charisma of a world leader (the Antichrist) and supported by a miracle-working False Prophet who heads the World Church.

Halfway through the tribulation period, war breaks out as greed grips the world. This war climaxes at the Armageddon Plain in a battle so awesome that, if not for the second coming of Jesus, the entire world would be destroyed. As Jesus returns, He subdues the foes and binds Satan, who has been the instigator of the evil.

Jesus then restores the earth over the next thousand years.

21

Man has engaged in many wars and battles over the ages, but none match the magnitude of the Battle of Armageddon predicted to occur sometime in the future.

The Bible Predicts a Final Nuclear War

Prophecies concerning the Battle of Armageddon are not found in one location in the Bible, but glimpses appear in both the Old and New Testament. When these fragments are pieced together, they form a powerful and clear story of the last war to occur on earth. In studying these prophecies remember, when God's Word speaks of the north, east, south, or west, the reference point is Israel. "In the north" means north of Israel.

After the rapture of the believers, the Antichrist will rise to power with great shrewdness and intelligence. He will destroy Christian converts and all who oppose him. He will be a great national leader empowered by Satan (Rev. 13:2). Read what the prophet Daniel was inspired to write in 553 B.C.:

And in the latter time of their kingdom, when the transgressors are come to the full, a king of fierce countenance, and understanding dark sentences, shall stand up. And his power shall be mighty, but not by his own power; and he shall destroy wonderfully, and shall prosper, and practise, and shall destroy the mighty and the holy people. (Dan 8:23-24)

During the first three-and-a-half years of the tribulation the Antichrist will bring the whole world to peace. John saw him as one of the four horsemen of the apocalypse.

> And I saw, and behold a white horse: And he that sat on him had a bow; and a crown was given unto him: and he went forth conquering, and to conquer. (Rev. 6:2)

At the midpoint of the seven-year tribulation period, the Antichrist will break his pledge and move in on Israel. He will enter the newly constructed temple and proclaim himself God (2 Thess. 2:3-4). From this vantage point he will have the authority to banish peace and bring anarchy to the earth. War and killing will break out everywhere.

To trace the details of the war that follows, we turn to the writings of two Hebrew prophets, Daniel and Ezekiel.

The Beginning of the War

First, Egypt attacks Israel and the Antichrist from the south. Then Russia (Gog) moves down from the north (Dan. 11:40). All of Russia's allies, a vast and awesome army, also roll down upon Israel like a storm and cover the land like a cloud (Ezek. 38:1-9).

Leading trade centers of Arabia question this attack and the destruction of cattle and robbing of riches (Ezek. 38:13). But Russia keeps moving with the strength and fury of a whirlwind; her vast army and navy rush in and probably kill the Antichrist. Now there's no stopping. Russia continues invading lands along the way and overthrowing governments, including Egypt, where the ancient treasures are captured. Libya and other nearby nations become their servants.

Russia suddenly halts. News from the east and north alarms her, and she returns to Israel in great anger, destroying as she goes (Dan. 11:40-45). This news is possibly the fact that the Antichrist has been miraculously revived, and is mustering his European nations to do battle. In Rev. 13:3 we see the Antichrist had a "deadly" wound. And in verse 12 the deadly wound is healed. Either the Antichrist is killed and brought back to life by the False Prophet or he is miraculously delivered from near death. However, the news could be from China to the east and the European powers to the north of Russia's stronghold in Libya.

The Defeat of Russia

God proclaims, "I am against you, Gog [Russia]. I will put hooks into your jaws and pull you to your doom" (Ezek. 38:3-4, TLB). Also pulled into this battle will be Iran, Black Africa, Libya, the Iron Curtain countries, and Russian Cossacks from the distant north (Ezek. 38:1-8). This is God's way of returning Russia to His own land, Israel (Lev. 25:23). Here He will destroy 85 percent of the Russian army in the mountainous region between the Dead Sea and the Mediterranean. Major cities in Russia and allied countries along the coast will burn (Ezek. 39:1-8).

The prophet Joel tells the same story, "I will remove these armies from the north and send them far away [to Egypt]; I will turn them back into the parched wastelands where they will die; half shall be driven into the Dead Sea and the rest into the Mediterranean, and then their rotting stench will rise upon the land" (Joel 2:20, TLB). God's intervention will likely be in the form of earthquakes, rain, and hail.

What happens to Egypt when God destroys Russia? For this answer we turn to the prophet Isaiah. The Egyptians begin to fight among themselves, and their spirit begins to fail. The Egyptian power has been scattered by Russia, so the Antichrist quickly takes over. The Nile does not rise to flood the fields, and crops wither and die. There is no fish to catch nor cotton and flax to make clothing and yarn. Great men and small are crushed and broken. Egypt as a nation is destroyed (Isa. 19:1-10). Again, Joel echoes the prophecy in Joel 3:19.

Under this pressure, Egypt's people will finally turn to God; He makes Christ known to them, and they are saved. Both Egypt and Iraq ally to Israel, and all three receive blessings (Isa. 19:21-25).

The exact order of events is difficult to establish. It does appear that over the last three and a half years of the Antichrist's reign these events occur: Antichrist, leader of the European powers, goes to Israel and proclaims himself to be God; Egypt attacks Israel; Russia attacks Israel and Egypt; Russia returns to Israel, where she and her allies are destroyed by God; Egypt, Israel, and Iraq ally, and the remaining world powers prepare for battle. Now there is a brief lull before the last and greatest battle of all.

The Battle of Armageddon

There is a stirring from the east. The Chinese powers muster their army of over 200 million soldiers (this quantity is possible today, according to an Associated Press release on April 24, 1964) for the final great war (Rev. 9:16). The great Euphrates River that divides the Orient from the Middle East suddenly dries up so the soldiers can cross (Rev. 16:12.) By now, the Antichrist has become so Satan-possessed that he and Satan become one (Rev. 13:2).

This Satanic power begins to confer with the remaining

rulers of the world to gather them for battle against the Lord. Soon all these armies of the world gather near a place called, in Hebrew, Armageddon, the Mountain of Megiddo (Rev. 16:16). Armageddon is the Plain of Esdraelon, just south of Nazareth, the only large, flat region in that part of the world where horses, men, and vehicles can do battle.

Although men and nations are physically at war at Armageddon, the forces behind them are Satanic. As the heat of the battle swells, it becomes a spiritual thrust so strong that Jesus himself leaves the right hand of God and enters the battlefield to mark the second coming of our Lord. And He will conquer (Rev. 17:14).

These armies of the world, gathered in the "Valley Where Jehovah Judges" (the meaning of Armageddon), will be punished there for the harm done throughout the centuries to God's land and people. "Announce this far and wide: Get ready for war! Constrict your best soldiers; collect all your armies. . . . Gather together and come, all nations everywhere. . . . for there I will sit to pronounce judgment on them all" (Joel 3:9-12, TLB).

> Multitudes, multitudes in the valley of decision: for the day of the Lord is near in the valley of decision. The sun and the moon shall be darkened, and the stars shall withdraw their shining. The Lord also shall roar out of Zion, and utter his voice from Jerusalem; and the heavens and the earth shall shake: but the Lord will be the hope of his people, and the strength of the children of Israel. (Joel 3:14-16)

A Nuclear Explosion
The earth and sky will begin to shake. Could this be

the result of a nuclear explosion in the vicinity? See how John described it in Rev. 16:17-21 (paraphrased):

When the seventh angel pours out his flask, a great electrical storm occurs. Then the greatest earthquake ever to occur splits Israel into three parts. So great will be this earthly rumble that cities all around the world will fall in heaps of rubble. Islands will vanish, and mountains will flatten out. So disrupted will be the atmosphere that hailstones weighing a hundred pounds will fall from the sky.

Two-thirds of all the nation of Israel will be cut off and die (Zech. 13:8). The Mount of Olives will be split, leaving a wide valley running from east to west. It is in this valley that the new Christian converts will be protected from the devastation (Zech. 14:3-5).

All the land of Judah will be leveled into one vast plain from the mighty destruction, but Jerusalem will be elevated. A nuclear explosion would be required to accomplish this. Here in Jerusalem the escaping Christians will find shelter and safety, never again to be cursed and destroyed (Zech. 14:10-11).

Non-Christians surviving the death blow will become like walking corpses. Their flesh will rot away, their eyes will shrivel in their sockets, and their tongues will decay in their mouths. Aren't these symptoms of nerve gases and fallout from a nuclear blast? Men will be seized with terror, panic-stricken, and will fight against each other in hand-to-hand combat. These same symptoms will appear upon the horses, mules, camels, donkeys, and all the other animals in the enemy camp (Zech. 14:12-15).

Destruction will come rapidly. In a moment, judgment will fall. All the wealth of the city will be gone. Israel as we know it today will disappear forever. Few will be left alive. Throughout the land the story is the same; only a remnant is left (Rev. 18:10-24). The earth will be broken down in utter collapse; everything will be lost, abandoned, and confused (Isa. 24:19).

The Second Coming

Just as the entire human race is on the verge of self-destruction at the Armageddon climax, Jesus Christ will appear in the heavens seated upon a white horse (Rev. 19:11). And all the armies of heaven will be mounted on white horses following Him. Jesus once told the high priest, "In the future you will see me . . . coming in the clouds of heaven" (Matt. 26:64).

The Antichrist too will see him and gather together the wounded governments of the earth and their armies to fight against Jesus. But to no avail, for the Antichrist and the False Prophet are captured by Christ and cast into the lake of fire, and their armies all killed (Rev. 19:19-21).

Then Jesus will mount the throne in the Temple and begin his thousand-year reign (Isa. 24:23). So will His prayer be fulfilled, "Thy kingdom come. Thy will be done in earth, as it is in heaven" (Matt.6:10).

22

The greatest desire lurking deep within the hearts of humans is to have the ability to defeat death.

How You Can Defeat Death

Any normal person can observe that all humans die. As a matter of fact, it is this fear of death that grips mankind today, causing great anxiety and unrest. The Bible tells us we need not fear death; God can grant eternal life. Does this sound like an exaggeration to you? It isn't. Here is how it works.

Faith, Hope, and Charity

Today we are unable to understand all the mysteries of the universe, "for now we see through a glass darkly." So the Bible tells us until we come "face to face" with Jesus (after death) we should abide in faith, hope, and charity (1 Cor. 13:12-13). What is implied here?

Faith is an attribute of God available to mankind. It allows us to know of things, such as the existence of God, that are not evident through the five physical senses. It is "the evidence of things not seen" (Heb. 11:1). To understand faith, read the eleventh chapter of Hebrews.

Charity is the love God had for man when He provided Jesus to be sacrificed on the cross to atone for our sin.

Hope is an expected desire, a feeling that what is wanted will occur. The Bible speaks of several things Christians hope for: righteousness, final rewards, the second coming of Jesus. But the greatest hope of the first century and of today is the hope to defeat death and live forever.

Paul said he wrote to Titus "in hope of eternal life,

which God, that cannot lie, promised before the world began" (Titus 1:2).

And Peter states:

> Blessed be the God and Father of our Lord Jesus Christ, which according to his abundant mercy hath begotten us again unto a lively hope by the resurrection of Jesus Christ from the dead. (1 Pet. 1:3)

God has made the promise of eternal life to us. He has shown that a resurrection into eternal life can occur. Then He tells us to abide in hope, awaiting our death and resurrection into eternal life.

Body, Soul, and Spirit

To understand just how God allows us to defeat death, we must first understand that man is composed of a body, soul, and spirit, as we read in 1 Thess. 5:23.

The *body* is the physical part that wears out after a few years and is usually cremated or buried in the ground.

The *soul* is the mind, will, and emotions. It is the Greek *psuche* (pronounced sū'-kay) or psyche. We have psychologists and psychiatrists who specialize in abnormalities of the psyche. The soul is not of material substance. It is the essence of "I." Upon death of the body, the soul of the believer enters into fellowship with Jesus (2 Cor. 5:8). The Bible says this is better for us; to live means a gain for Christ as we continue to bear fruit, but to die is a personal gain (Phil. 1:21-24). Our soul is what gives us our feelings and our intelligence; it motivates us.

The *spirit* is something different. With the spirit we do not "feel"; we "know." In its simplest terms the spirit is the residence of God in man. It is that point at which God touches man and lets him "know." It is the union of

God and man. The spirit is not of material substance, and is apart from the body at death (James 2:26).

Just as God is of a triune nature—Father, Son, and Holy Spirit—so is man triune, being created in His image. Just as the Godhead is made up of three Persons, so man, being one person, is made up of three dimensions—body, soul, and spirit.

While Jesus is the bodily manifestation of the Godhead, He is still a human being and thus possesses His own body, soul, and spirit as do all humans. Let us see how this trinity in Jesus separated at His death.

As Jesus was hanging on the cross, He told another, also condemned to die, "Today you will see me in paradise" (Luke 23:43). Jesus was saying their *spirits* would meet in heaven immediately after death. But what happened to Jesus' soul?

At death, the soul of Jesus "descended first into the lower parts of the earth" (Eph. 4:9). That He (His soul) separated and descended is also verified in 1 Pet. 3:19, Ps. 16:10, and Matt. 12:40.

So where does that leave Jesus' body? In the grave of course (Luke 23:53). Recall that Pilate's soldiers went to the tomb the second day, inspected it to be sure the body was still there, then placed the cord and Roman seal over its entrance (Matt. 27:62-66).

Thus we see that at death, Jesus' trinity (body, soul, and spirit) divided, only to reunite on the third day when He appeared to Mary at the tomb.

When a Christian Dies

For the Christian there is no task to perform in the "lower parts of the earth," so at death, while the fleshly body rests in the grave, both the soul and spirit ascend to heaven to be with God. In the Apostle John's vision of heaven he actually saw living souls in full conscious-ness—souls whose fleshly bodies had been killed during the end-time tribulation period—Christian converts after the rapture.

And when he had opened the fifth seal, I saw under the altar the souls of them that were slain for the word of God, and for the testimony which they held. (Rev. 6:9)

In 2 Cor. 5:1-4 Paul writes that when we die and our earthly bodies dissolve we, our soul and spirit, are given new spiritual bodies not made with hands.

For we know that if our earthly house of this taber-nacle were dissolved, we have a building of God, an house not made with hands, eternal in the heavens. (2 Cor. 5:1)

That this spiritual body is given to us *immediately* is substantiated by the fact that Paul reassures us that we will not be found naked during the intermediate state between death and the "resurrection of the body" or rapture we speak of when we recite the Apostle's Creed. Read how Paul puts it.

For in this we groan, earnestly desiring to be clothed upon with our house which is from heaven: If so be that being clothed we shall not be found naked. (2 Cor. 5:2-3)

That the soul and spirit, both invisible, intangible entities, are immediately given an identifiable, spiritual body is further proven when we read of the recognizable bodies of Abraham and the beggar Lazarus as *seen* by the rich man—all who had died in the flesh.

And it came to pass, that when the beggar died, and was carried by the angels into Abraham's bosom: the rich man also died, and was buried; And in hell he lifted up his eyes, being in torments, and seeth Abraham afar off, and Lazarus in his bosom. (Luke 16:22-23)

Peter, James, and John on the Mount of Transfiguration, being alive and in the flesh, actually *saw* the bodies of Moses and Elijah, who had been dead in the flesh many years (Matt. 17:1-3). And Jesus says, "And whosoever liveth and believeth in me shall never die . . ." (John 11:26), inferring we are never disembodied.

Collectively, these Scriptures substantiate the fact that at death our soul and spirit are immediately given a recognizable, spiritual body, leaving one to wonder what happens to our fleshly body.

Our fleshly body is just a shell that makes us aware of being in the world; *it* breathes, *we* don't; *it* aches, *we* don't. *It* is a shell that rots away in time, ". . . for dust thou art, and unto dust shalt thou return" (Gen. 3:19). But *it* is not us. We are a living soul that lives in a body and has a spirit. And since the soul and spirit go with God at death, the grave gets nothing but the shell, the body. We need not fear death, for we will be present with God (2 Cor. 5:8). Now here is what happens to those fleshly bodies.

The Hope of the Flesh

The Bible says our flesh "shall rest in hope" (Ps. 16:9). Hope after death is only for the flesh, the body. The soul and spirit are already with God. They depart as soon as our physical bodies die. Our hope is that our present bodies will someday resurrect and reunite with our soul and spirit. To prove that this can be done, God caused it to happen with Jesus and provided hundreds of eyewitnesses to testify that Jesus indeed defeated death bodily, and that He is only the first of many to follow (1 Cor. 15:12-23).

God has filled us with peace and joy in this new belief, this good news that lets us abound in hope through the power of the Holy Spirit (Rom. 15:13). God wants us to live an abundant life; that is one of the reasons Jesus came (John 10:10). He doesn't want His people fearing death. We are to abound in the fruit of the spirit: love, joy, peace, patience, gentleness, goodness, and faith (Gal. 5:22). How can we bear such beautiful fruit if we are diseased with the fear of death?

Our hope is for "a resurrection of the dead, both of the just and unjust" (Acts 24:15). The Bible says the hope of the righteous Christian is gladness, whereas the non-believer's hope leads to disappointment (Prov. 10:28). The hope of the wicked leads to eternal death (Job 11:20). In other words the Christian's hope, to bodily defeat death, will be rewarded.

When will this resurrection take place? No one knows exactly, but God has given us signs to know the approximate time. "But ye, brethren, are not in darkness, that that day should overtake you as a thief" (1 Thess. 5:4).

Behold, I shew you a mystery; We shall not all sleep, but we shall be changed, In a moment, in the twinkling of an eye, at the last trump: for the trumpet shall sound, and the dead shall be raised incorruptible, and we shall be changed. For this corruptible must put on incorruptible, and this mortal must put on immortality. So when this corruptible shall have put on incorruption, and this mortal shall have put on immortality, then shall be brought to pass the saying that is written, Death is swallowed up in victory. O death, where is thy sting? O grave, where is thy victory? (1 Cor. 15:51-55)

Does this all sound illogical? So does the birth of a baby, the fruition of a tree, and the germination of a seed. God has already shown us He can do it, by raising Jesus from the dead. And He promises us He will do it again at the second coming of Christ. The Bible admits the resurrection is a mystery but profoundly states that this mystery is now made manifest to Christians everywhere. Here is the solution to the mystery: "Christ in you, the hope of glory" (Col. 1:26-27).

Do you hope your body will resurrect and defeat death the way Jesus' did? Christ in you is the secret. Christ said, "Behold, I stand at the door and knock: if any man hear my voice, and open the door, I will come in to him, and will sup with him, and he with me" (Rev. 3:20).

The next time you pray, tell Christ you believe in Him and accept Him, and His Spirit will enter your spirit. It is as simple as that. You probably won't feel a thing and may go away feeling your prayers were unheard. But God's Word promises if you will do just that, a change will be made in your destiny, and you can start abounding in *hope* and the *joy* of being a Christian, for you will have already defeated the sting of death. When you die, the real you (your soul and spirit) will go immediately to God, where it will receive an identifiable, spiritual body, while your fleshly body will rest in hope for a few years, to be reunited later when Christ reenters our atmosphere. Where is the fear?

Conclusion

It is the nature of God to provide for the people of this earth a *sufficiency* for their needs. He has provided not an *overabundance*, but a *sufficiency* of food, natural resources, space, speed of travel, and rate of reproduction. Even our *rate of discovery* is sufficient. God has given us an intellect that allows us to uncover secrets of the universe when we need them and when we can handle them. Consider man's mastery of fire, electricity, atomic energy, and space travel. These were brought to light due to a God-set *rate of discovery*.

Likewise, the evidence God has given us in support of the Bible and all its teachings is *sufficient*. If it were overabundant, absolute, and all-convincing, then we would not need the ministry of the Holy Spirit to convict fallen citizens of the earth and turn their hearts to God, for all the world would believe.

The most obvious conclusion after seeing the mountain of evidence in support of God's Word is that it is *sufficient* to stimulate man's faith in God. God has carefully planned it this way, for He wants His children to turn to Him *by faith*, not merely by fact. Today, Jesus sits at the right hand of God and serves as intercessor for our prayers, awaiting the day when He will return to the earth; the Holy Spirit resides with us, convicting, teaching, helping us to grow in faith; the angels surround us with a hedge of protection. But none force us to believe anything.

While impressive arguments against God, the Bible, and all its teachings are still postulated by some in the community of the "intellectually enlightened," God wants every Christian and non-Christian, sooner or later, to have the opportunity to study His evidence of fulfilled prophecy, typology, and the historical record of the archaeologist. And, accepting the nudgings of the Holy Spirit in his conscience, turn *by faith* to God and receive His word and abide by its teachings. It is to this end that God ministers to man.

Selected Bibliography

Albright, William F. *Archaeology of Palestine and the Bible.* New York: Revell, 1932.

Albright, William F. *From the Stone Age to Christianity.* Baltimore: Johns Hopkins Press, 1946.

Bloomfield, Arthur E. *Before the Last Battle—Armageddon.* Minneapolis, Minn.: Bethany Fellowship, 1971.

Bruce, F. F. *The Books and the Parchments.* Rev. ed. Westwood: Fleming H. Revell Co., 1963.

Bruce, F. F. *The New Testament Documents: Are They Reliable?* Downers Grove, Ill.: Inter-Varsity Press, 1964.

Burrows, Millar. *The Dead Sea Scrolls.* New York: Viking Press, 1955.

Collett, Sydney. *All About the Bible.* Old Tappan, N.J.: Fleming H. Revell Co., no date.

Danielou, Jean. *The Dead Sea Scrolls and Primitive Christianity.* New York: Mentor Omega Books, 1958.

Davies, A. Powell. *The Meaning of the Dead Sea Scrolls.* New York: Mentor Books, 1956.

Davis, John J. *Biblical Numerology.* Winona Lake, Ind.: BMH Books, 1968.

Dickason, C. Fred. *Angels, Elect and Evil.* Chicago: Moody Press, 1975.

Free, Joseph P. *Archaeology and Bible History.* Wheaton, Ill.: Scripture Press, 1969.

Gaebelein, A.C. *What The Bible Says About Angels.* Grand Rapids, Mich.: Baker Book House, 1975.

Gilbert, George Holley. *The Student's Life of Paul.* New York: The Macmillan Co., 1902.

Goodspeed, Edgar J. *How Came The Bible?* New York: Abingdon-Cokesbury Press, 1940.

Graham, Billy. *Angels.* New York: Doubleday, 1975.

Habershon, Ada R. *The Study of Types.* Grand Rapids,

Mich.: Kregel Publications, 1974.

Hefley, James C. *Adventures With God.* Grand Rapids, Mich.: Zondervan Publishing House, 1967.

Hefley, James C. *What's So Great About the Bible.* Elgin, Ill.: David C. Cook Publishing Co., 1969.

Hoyt, Herman A. *The Revelation of the Lord Jesus Christ.* Winona Lake, Ind.: Brethren Missionary Herald Co., 1966.

Huegel, F.J. *The Cross Through the Scriptures.* Grand Rapids, Mich.: Zondervan Publishing House, 1966.

Humber, Thomas. *The Fifth Gospel: The Miracle of the Holy Shroud.* New York: Pocket Books, 1974.

James, M.R. (Translator). *The Apocryphal New Testament.* New York: Oxford University Press, 1942.

Jauncey, James H. *Science Returns to God.* Grand Rapids, Mich.: Zondervan Publishing House, 1961.

Jauncey, James H. *Why We Believe.* Cincinnati, Ohio: Standard Publishing, 1969.

Keller, Werner. *The Bible As History.* Bantam Books, 1956.

Kenyon, Frederic G. *The Bible and Modern Scholarship.* London: John Murray, 1948.

Kirban, Salem. *Guide to Survival.* Wheaton, Ill.: Tyndale House, 1968.

LaHaye, Tim. *The Beginning of the End.* Wheaton, Ill.: Tyndale House, 1973.

Leaming, Charles M. *I Saw Angels.* St. Petersburg, Fla.: Faith Temple Ministries, 1976.

Lindsey, Hal. *The Late Great Planet Earth.* Grand Rapids, Mich.: Zondervan Publishing House, 1970.

Lindsey, Hal. *There's A New World Coming.* Santa Ana, Calif.: Vision House Publishers, 1973.

Little, Paul E. *Know Why You Believe.* New York:

Pyramid Publications, 1973.

McDowell, Josh. *Evidence That Demands a Verdict.* San Bernardino, Calif.: Campus Crusade for Christ, 1972.

McDowell, Josh. *More Evidence That Demands a Verdict.* San Bernardino, Calif.: Campus Crusade for Christ, 1975.

McGee, J. Vernon. *The Empty Tomb.* Glendale, Calif.: G/L Publications, 1968.

McIntosh and Twyman (Translators). *The Archko Volume.* New Canaan, Conn.: Keats Publishing, Inc., 1975.

Montgomery, John Warwick. *How Do We Know There Is a God?* Minneapolis, Minn.: Bethany Fellowship, 1973.

Morison, Frank. *Who Moved the Stone.* Grand Rapids, Mich.: Zondervan Publishing House, no date.

Morris, Henry M. *Many Infallible Proofs.* San Diego: Creation-Life Publishers, 1974.

Navarra, Fernand. *Noah's Ark: I Touched It.* Plainfield, N.J.: Logos, 1974.

Orr, Edwin J. *100 Questions About God.* Glendale, Calif.: G/L Publications, 1967.

Parsons, Elmer E. *Witness to the Resurrection.* Grand Rapids, Mich.: Baker Book House, 1967.

Pfeiffer, Charles F. *The Dead Sea Scrolls and the Bible.* Grand Rapids, Mich.: Baker Book House, 1969.

Phillips, Bob. *When the Earth Quakes.* Wheaton, Ill.: Key Publishers, Inc., 1973.

Potter, Charles Francis. *The Lost Years of Jesus Revealed.* Greenwich, Conn.: Fawcett Publications, Inc. 1958.

Reid, James. *Does Science Confront the Bible?* Grand Rapids, Mich.: Zondervan Publishing House, 1971.

Ridenour, Fritz [editor]. *Who Says?* Glendale, Calif.: G/L Publications, 1967.

Rinaldi, Peter M. *It Is the Lord: A Study of the Shroud of Christ.* New York: Warner Books Inc., 1972.

Scroggie, W. Graham. *Is the Bible the Word of God?* Chicago: Moody Press, 1922.

Smith, Wilbur M. *The Biblical Doctrine of Heaven.* Chicago: Moody Press, 1968.

Stoner, Peter. *Science Speaks.* Chicago: Moody Press, 1963.

Thompson, J.A. *The Bible and Archaeology.* Grand Rapids, Mich.: Wm. B. Eerdmans Publishing Co., 1972.

Torrey, R.A. *Difficulties In the Bible.* Chicago: Moody Press, no date.

Vollmer, Philip. *The Modern Student's Life of Christ.* Old Tappan, N.J.: Fleming H. Revell Company, 1912.

Vos, Howard F. [editor]. *Can I Trust the Bible?* New York: Pyramid Publications, 1972.

White, John Wesley. *Re-entry.* Grand Rapids, Mich.: Zondervan Publishing House, 1970.

Whyte, Alexander. *The Apostle Paul.* Grand Rapids, Mich.: Baker Book House, 1977.

Wolvoord, John F. and John E. *Armageddon.* Grand Rapids, Mich.: Zondervan Publishing House, 1974.